Girl Fix Your Crown

Tresniece Perry

For information contact:
PO Box 518
Temple Hills, Md 20757
http://www.simplytresniece.com

ISBN: 978-1-7327674-1-6
Library of Congress Control Number: 2018911119

Printed in the United States of America by Vision to Fruition
Publishing
www.vision-fruition.com

Foreword

Welcome *Queen*. Welcome to a place that will require you to do a self-inventory check. A place that will reaffirm, confirm, and alert you to the fact you are a *Queen*. Yes, reader you are a *Queen* not simply because I, the author of this book says it but because God Himself ordained it. God, the One who created you and made you a masterpiece, He is the one that knows you as a *Queen*. Throughout this book I will refer to you by the name God calls you; *Queen*. Every time you see your name it's a reminder of who God created you to be.

This book was birthed out of God's reminder to me that I am a *Queen*. No matter what life has thrown at me, no matter where I have been or what state I am currently in, I am still a *Queen*. This is book is about redefining the term *Queen* and allowing you permission to WALK in the knowledge that you are a *Queen*.

This book will require you to reject any lie you believed about yourself by first requiring you to go from *Empty to Full*. Once God has taken you on the journey of emptying you, He is going to request you to *Grant Pardons* to people who caused offense. Next God will challenge the *Victim Mindset* which prevents you from becoming the *Queen* you are destined to be. Once God has dealt with this mindset He will address your *Queen Mindset*. This mindset will challenge everything you have believed about yourself and God. *Queen*, in order to Fix Your Crown, you must first understand and embrace that *Your Worthy* of all God has for you.

After addressing this area God will check your vision to ensure you are living a *Faith Based Reality*. There is a King who was created just for you, but you need to know how to *Date Like a Queen*. This book will have you look at your relationships to see who makes up your *Queen Court* and their impact on your life. Finally, God is going to present you with *A Gift Fit for a Queen*.

It's my prayer that once you complete this book God will have removed all fears, doubt, and shame that take away from who God intends you to be.

No matter what you are a still a *Queen* and its time you took your rightful place. Your past is not a factor, nor does your present state factor into how God sees you. Your future is still being built. All God needs you to do is trust this journey. Take notes, cry if you must, but let this book minister to you. Allow God to go into those areas you have kept hidden. Grant God access to your secrets, your past, your present, your future. Know there is **PURPOSE** in your pain, **PURPOSE** in your tears, **PURPOSE** in the shame. *Queen*, there is a **PURPOSE** God has for your life and this book is your first look at it. So, starting today Girl Fix Your Crown, for there is work to be done.

My Prayer for You

I pray God will keep and cover you all day and all night

I pray HIS favor will go before you to be a light

I pray to HIS strength will keep you in the midst to know the greater days
are ahead

I pray you know HIS love in ways you can't explain

I pray God forever shines HIS grace upon you

I pray you understand the depth of God's love

I pray you know that it's truly sent from God above

I pray for the **Queen** you are today and the one yet to come

I pray your latter shall be greater than what you've known it to be

I pray you see yourself the way God sees you

I pray you always know God has a plan for you

I pray you know His plan will see you through

I pray heaven shines upon you and all your dreams come true

Queen, above all of this I pray for the real you

Chapters

Empty to Full

Empty: 1. a: containing nothing

b: not occupied or inhabited

2. a: lacking reality, substance, meaning, or value

Full: 1. containing as much or as many as is possible or normal

2. a: complete especially in detail, number, or duration

b: lacking restraint, check or qualification

c: having all distinguishing characteristics: enjoying all authorized rights and privileges

d: not lacking in anything essential

Psalm 63:1-3

O God, You are my God; with deepest longing I will seek You; My soul [my life, my very self] thirsts for You, my flesh longs and sighs for You, in a dry and weary land where there is no water. [2] So I have gazed upon You in the sanctuary, to see Your power and Your glory. [3] Because Your lovingkindness is better than life, my lips shall praise You.

Amplified Bible (AMP)

*E*ver wanted to escape the countless thoughts in your head?

Ever wanted to outrun a painful memory? Ever wanted to get far away from reality and be in a place where none of the cares of the world mattered? A place where no one knew of your mistakes or failures? A place where you could create the perfect new identity for yourself?

This was me in 2004, when I got accepted into college in a totally different state. At the age of 24 I decided I needed a "break" from the life I had known. I wanted to be some place where I knew no one. A place where no one knew I was a Christian. A place where I set the rules and could be anyone I wanted to be. I was tired of doing it the right way and I wanted to be free.

So, I applied and got into this very nice college and quickly realized no matter how many miles I moved away. No matter how many drinks I had or parties I attended, when I got back to the dorm room, the same emptiness that sent me running to another state met me there. The same emptiness I had at home in Maryland now traveled with me as an unwanted guest in my heart.

I was frustrated because my plan to be "happy and full" failed and I was now stuck in this new place still dealing with the issues of my heart. In this broken place it became easier to sleep than to attend class. I made excuses as to why the grades I was getting were the lowest in my history of schooling. I embraced the fact that I was just getting by and was okay with it.

Coming home at the end of that first school year only added to the emptiness I felt deep down inside. Instead of telling anyone, I simply fell back in to the routine of church activities, smiling at the right time, and being the best version of me, while quietly, dying on the inside.

The problem was that no matter how many bible studies I attended or how many times I shouted, my heart still hurt from the pain of being rejected. My heart still hurt from remembering I had been molested. The scars from the self-hate and no esteem had not yet healed. The shame of my body was still an issue. The guilt from having sex before marriage was still present. My heart was in shambles, but I did my best to smile through it and pretend everything was alright in my world.

Queen, does this story sound familiar to you? How many times have you smiled when your heart hurt or said you were fine when you were broken? Does this story reflect your inner thoughts? Many times, we as women push down or ignore our heart. We block out the signs of heart damage with the hopes that attending another conference will heal only what God can heal. We "pray away" the symptoms of heart disease believing another solo in choir will remove it.

Your heart, one of the most precious parts of your body, is often the most overlooked. God thought so much of your heart He took special care in hiding it behind other organs to ensure its protection. For its protection, God hid it behind the ribs and the lungs. God even; when He was creating us; knew the importance of protecting the heart. Countless scriptures were written giving warning to the neglect of your heart and effects of it.

Tresniece Perry

Heart Check-Up

How is it possible for the love of God to flow out of your heart when your heart is full of anger, bitterness, forgiveness, hate, depression, doubt, shame, etc.? How can we shower people with the love of God when all that is left are pieces of what should be a heart? *Queen*, how can you pray for God to send you a real, true and honest love when you have spent a lifetime giving your heart to people who have mishandled and misused it?

The condition of your heart is visible even when you are not talking. Your words, your actions, and the people you surround yourself with all reflect your heart. Your outlook on life and of others reflect your heart in ways your words will never have too.

Proverbs 27:19
Just as water mirrors your face, so your face mirrors your heart.
The Message (MSG) Bible

No matter how successful you are or how many likes you are able to get on social media the truth is *your heart is the truest reflection of you.* If given enough time *Queen* your heart will expose your truest thoughts and emotions. It will show how vulnerable you are and the impact of the rejection. It will show the signs of the failed marriage or the abortion.

It shows the strains of the disappointments and failures. At the weirdest times your heart will expose itself to anyone with a listening ear. It will show up when you are angry. It will show up just when you think you've mastered the art burying it all deep inside. It will show up in your health. It will show up in relationships. Make no mistake what is in the heart will find its way out.

Luke 6:45

People are known in this same way. Out of the virtue stored in their hearts, good and upright people will produce good fruit. But out of the evil hidden in their hearts, evil ones will produce what is evil. For the overflow of what has been stored in your heart will be seen by your fruit and will be heard in your words.
The Passion Translation (TPT)

Heart's Impact

During a conversation with my Pastor (aka Mama) she said, "Baby girl, we all have a life theme." She went on to explain throughout our lives God allows different things to happen to shape our ministry. Let me explain. God is not looking to make our lives hard. He allows certain trials to push us into our **PURPOSE** and **DESTINY.** The saying *My Story His Glory* is a true testament to the way God intends for you to live your life.

Meaning everything you've experienced in this life is for His Glory. Your good days are for His Glory, your bad days are for His Glory and your 'oh my' days are for His Glory too! Everything that happens is not only for His glory but it's creating your life theme that will flow into the **PURPOSE** and **DESTINY** God handcrafted for a life theme in your life.

Tresniece Perry

Stop for a moment and think about your life (no matter how long or short it may have been). Think about the place where you seem to always have an attack. For me it was matters of the heart. When I looked over my life my attacks all revolved around the heart. The issues with my dad-matters of the heart, issues with relationships-matters of the heart, issues with self-esteem- matters of the heart. My greatest struggle has been to give unconditional love and to receive it.

Hidden under all the other cares of this world were matters of the heart. It's possible for a perfectly healthy-looking person to pass away because of heart issues. Why? Because matters of the heart are hidden until they are put under the correct spotlight and fully examined. If God was to examine your heart today *Queen* what would He find?

Queen there will be signs of trouble unless they are addressed. Issues gradually become worst until either they are exposed and addressed, or the heart simply gives out from the stress of working too hard.

Looking at these moments I now recognize that each of these situations were each meant to destroy the very thing I needed to do; what God had called me to do. Each attack stripped away my ability to show love to others (I was becoming bitter and jaded), my ability to receive love from others (I questioned everything someone said), and finally my ability to receive God's love (how can I minister something that I wasn't allowing in).

Often, what makes these attacks so deadly is there are no physical marks left. Looking at me no one (not even me) could see the damage that had been done. It was not until a thorough evaluation was conduct by a specialist, that I was able to see the damage that was left behind.

Many of you reading this right now can relate. You go through life daily never knowing the deadly impact your heart has suffered. Therefore, you struggle to relate to your husband. You struggle in accepting God's love because of the damage from the lack of love from your birth father. The consistent breaking of your heart because you loved someone who was not equipped to love you God's way left your heart in pieces. Under the mask of being happy and living this perfect life your heart strains to function in the way in which God created it.

Your ability to show love is directly related to the status of your heart. You want better relationships with others, mend your heart. You want a relationship with God, get your heart healed. Tired of always being angry, let God deal with the issues of your heart. I cannot stress this enough, but everything is connected to your heart. Without a beating heart a person cannot live.

Heart Surgery: The Process

Psalm 147:3
He heals the wounds of every shattered heart.
The Passion Translation (TPT)

Earlier in the chapter I mentioned that we must allow healing. We must be willing to go through a process to allow God to do His work in us and through us. This part is what I like to call "heart surgery." When it's time for a patient to have open heart surgery the patient is sent to a specialist. They don't send a heart patient to an ear, nose and throat doctor and expect a positive outcome. **Queen**, why do you keep allowing people who are equipped with fixing your heart access to your heart?

No, the patient is sent to a doctor who has the necessary training to perform a surgery where the smallest detail means life or death. This is exactly what God is doing in this portion of the book. God understands, for you to move to the next chapter of your life He needs to perform heart surgery, but you **Queen** must be willing to go through the process.

In this process God is like that skilled surgeon, He's taking time to pay close attention to the smallest details. God takes the time to deal with thoughts, behaviors, actions, and beliefs that have impacted the heart. Skillfully as only a specialist can God goes in and repairs the areas of the heart that are damaged and any surrounding areas that may have been affected by the damaged area. God removes the damaged parts of the heart, thus creating a new route for His love to flow through.

Luke 3:9
Even now God's axe of judgment is poised to chop down your barren tree right down to its roots! And every tree that does not produce good fruit will be leveled and thrown into the fire. The Passion Translation (TPT)

In other words, *God goes to the root cause* of the drinking, the root cause of the drug abuse, the root cause of the self-harm, the root cause of sexing, the root cause of the fear and shame, the root cause of the guilt, and the root cause of it all. **God is intent** on you not just being healed on the surface but completely and totally healed; mind, body and soul. The areas of your heart that are stopping you from bearing the fruits of being the *Queen* you are called and created to be is what God is after.

It's during this process God up roots everything that goes against His promise and destroys it. The process will allow God to pull back the layers of pain, hurt, anger, fear, disappoint, shame, guilt, and fears to expose the root cause of the blockage.

Queens, stop for a moment and think what your roots are? What are the reasons why you are angry or mad all the time? What are the reasons one man is never enough for you? It's ok if you don't know. With you being open to the move of God during the time of reading this book, God will expose the areas that you have kept hidden if you allow Him to.

Take a moment and write down the areas (if you know them) if not you can simply write "God what are my roots?" and then listen for the Holy Spirit to tell you:

_____

_____

_____

_____

_____

_____

_____

_____

_____

_____

The process is not a comfortable one. It's a time of great pruning and the trying of one's faith. It's during this time some dear relationships may end. The vices that got you through once (men, drugs, alcohol) will not work. During this process it's seems that God is breaking you down to leave you but that is so far from the truth.

What's really happening is Gods placing you directly in the fire. This fire will dissolve the residue of your past mistakes, the lingering doubts and fears, the dark places where unforgiveness and hurt are and the deep places of the heart that were broken.

Queen look at it this way, God is taking gold (that's you) from the dirty place (that's life) and placing it in the fire (your process) so that all the dirt can be burned away, and its real value and worth can shine through. So, all that's left is a valuable piece of gold (you). When you pull gold from the mines, you know it's worth, even though, in its current state it does not reflect its worth. The fire changes the outside of the gold to match the inside of the gold and that is what God wants for you.

Malachi 3:3
He will sit as a refiner and purifier of silver, and He will purify the sons of Levi [the priests], and refine them like gold and silver, so that they may present to the Lord [grain] offerings in righteousness.
Amplified Bible (AMP)

The process is important because without it you would still be walking around looking like the dirt you were found in. The process has the power to *reshape, remold, and conform* you into the **Queen** GOD created you to be.

That's the thing about God, He does not see you in your messed-up state, He sees you as the person He created you to be. He is not worried about the place you are currently in because He knows where you are headed is so much better.

Just like when Jesus told Peter, the devil desires to sift you like wheat. He called Peter by his old name because the way he was acting was reflecting Simon, the old Peter. In that portion of scripture Peter, the man who walked with Jesus was missing in action.

By the end of the scripture Jesus again referred to Peter as Peter by telling him (Peter), He (Jesus) was praying for him. In other words, you are tripping right now but I know what's on the inside of you. I know what changes have been made on the inside of you and even though right now you are out of character, I know the PURPOSE AND DESTINY on the inside of you will win and Peter will emerge again. **(Luke 22:31-34)**. *Queen*, when God sees you, He does not see the drunk or the addict He sees a *Queen*.

Remember God told David he would be king long before he became King. David went through a process that had him hiding in caves and acting like a crazy person before he became king. He killed a giant with a stone, long before he became a king. It was his process. You too *Queen* will have your process.

Stop comparing your process with someone else's. What God sends you through is for the place He is taking you to not someone else. Stop wishing you had this person or that person's life because you don't know their process. The truth is if God required you to endure what they endured, you may not survive it. Rest assured, God will fulfill His promise to you but, in the meantime, trust the process.

God is clear when He says, *"in order to be filled one must first be WILLING to be emptied."* If a glass is already filled with pollution and someone goes and pours clean water into the polluted water, it's a waste. If the goal was to have clean water the polluted water first needs to be emptied and the residue still attached to the glass washed before what I pour in can be useable.

Luke 5:36-39
No one cuts up a fine silk scarf to patch old work clothes; you want fabrics that match. And you don't put wine in old, cracked bottles; you get strong, clean bottles for your fresh vintage wine. And no one who has ever tasted fine aged wine prefers unaged wine.
The Message (MSG)

Queen, for God to perform this surgery you must first be willing to be emptied so that God can fill you and equip you to do the work your created to do. At some point in your life *Queen* we all will to be emptied. We all must allow God to go inside and change any and everything that is slowing your progress.

I once heard someone say, "be careful saying yes because it may cost you something". Being willing to be emptied is saying **YES to God** and His plans for **Your** life. It's saying God I give you permission to go in and remove everything (attachments, pain, lost love, fears, rejection, shame guilt, etc.) and fill me up with YOU. It's saying God I know this process might not always feel good, but

I know it will be worth it. It says God have your way. It's after the emptying process we are truly ready for the master's use. After your filling is complete now you are an open vessel that can be used.

Heart's Impact

Luke 22:31-32

Simon, stay on your toes. Satan has tried his best to separate all of you from me, like chaff from wheat. Simon, I've prayed for you in particular that you not give in or give out. When you have come through the time of testing, turn to your companions and give them a fresh start.
The Message (MSG)

Queen take a moment and think about what area have you struggled the most with. Below in the space provided write your life's theme. Now if one does not come to mind it's okay. Just pause and ask God what your life theme is.
My life theme is:

_____

Once God gives you the life theme your next question for God is how you want me to use it. How can this theme impact your kingdom for the better? Remember this journey is not solely for you. Once you get the answer make sure you take a moment to help another *Queen* find her life's theme. Real *Queen*s help to fix the crowns of other *Queen*s.

There is a story in the Bible where Jesus is talking to His disciple Peter (whose former name was Simon). In this portion of scripture Jesus tells Peter the devil has desired you with the intent of sifting you like wheat. In other words, the devil asked for permission to beat on Peter until all that was in him was separated from its root.

Know the devil must ask God for permission to bother you. Once you accept Jesus as your Lord and Savior (if you need to do this check out the last chapter of the book) you are then entered into God's family. As a result, God grants permission for things to happen in your life. Meaning if God allowed it to come to you, everything you need to succeed God has already put on the inside of you.

Back to the story, Jesus tells Peter, BUT I have prayed for you. This is the same for you. Jesus is sitting beside God praying for you. Praying you make it through this test. Praying that you don't give up on God and His promises. Praying for you that you see this thing to the end. He is praying for you to finish the race.

Finally, Jesus tells Peter once you have gone through what you have gone through go back and get your brother. **Queen** this is the same for you. Once you have gone through the trial and allowed God to heal you, go back and get another **Queen** that is struggling. Therefore, we tell our stories because in telling your story someone else will know they can make it. Another **Queen** knows there is light at the end of the tunnel.

Now, that you have allowed the specialist to come in and do His work there is another area God seeks to deal with. God is requesting you to grant pardons to those who have damaged your heart.

Granting Pardons

Forgiveness

Forgiveness: the act of pardoning somebody for a mistake or wrongdoing; the tendency to forgive offenses readily and easily

Mark 11:25
Whenever you [a]stand praying, if you have anything against anyone, forgive him [drop the issue, let it go], so that your Father who is in heaven will also forgive you your transgressions and wrongdoings [against Him and others]. Amplified Bible (AMP)

There was this lady working in a call center named Mary.

Mary's very first call of the day was from an upset customer. No matter what Mary did the caller was rude and nasty. Even after apologizing for the companies mistake the customer was still irate. Finally, the caller just hung up the phone on the Mary.

Tresniece Perry

Mary was upset and proceeded to tell her coworker what happened on the phone. Even after this call Mary's day continued and she took more calls but all throughout the morning her mind stayed on her first caller. Finally, Mary got a break but instead of enjoying the break she tells another coworker what happened on her first call.

At lunch time, she did the same thing, Mary told a new set of coworkers about her first caller. The morning turns into the afternoon and when she gets her afternoon break, you guessed it Mary told a different coworker about her morning call from that morning. It's finally time to go home but Mary is still upset and stuck on her caller from the morning.

Mary arrives home and when her husband asked about her day, she goes on and on about her first call of the morning. Mary then starts her evening activities but the caller from the morning is never far from her mind or her emotions. Even as Mary laid down, the morning caller was still with Mary.

The next morning comes and Mary prepares for work and her prayer is: "God, please don't let me have another morning like yesterday. Let me have a good first call today". Now in this story the caller is never given a name. We don't even know the exact reason for the call that morning other than it something the company did. But what happened, the rude caller spent an entire day with Mary.

She took every break Mary took. She ate lunch and dinner with Mary; she went home with Mary, met her husband and slept in the same bed with him. She took a shower with Mary and even had a part of Mary's evening and morning prayers. For only one encounter with Mary, the lady sure did become the uninvited guest in Mary's life.

The point of the story is to show you how things can have such a powerful hold on you. The thing that makes unforgiveness unreachable for you can be like Mary's caller. That thing has gotten through school with you. It has helped to raise your kids. It has been the uninvited guest at your wedding and divorce. It was there when you got your first job. It was there when you attended church services and waited for you when you left. It has been present for every high and low moment in your life. This is what unforgiveness looks like. It can be the uninvited guest in your life that, without the right weapons, will never leave.

The Power of Unforgiveness

How many times have you said to a person or to yourself that you forgive them? Only to discover all those emotions are lying dormant below the surface. Maybe it was a song that played while you were in the store and instantly you became that broken little girl again. It could have been a picture in the family photo album which reminds you of how he violated you. It could be a smell in the air that smells just like him. What about your child, who looks just like your ex-husband, who is a constant reminder of your failed marriage.

It does not matter what triggers the memory. What matters is you becoming free from the bondage of the offense. Unforgiveness, no matter the reason is like going into the pool for a swim, tying a weight around your ankle, yet expecting to be able to swim.

Tresniece Perry

It's invisible to the naked eye, but it has the power to affect every area of your life, every relationship (new and old), and cause you to stop growing. It has the power to prevent you from becoming the **Queen** you were meant to be. Unforgiveness is bondage. It sets a barrier between God, your **PURPOSE,** and your **DESTINY.** Unforgiveness, when left unchecked can destroy marriages. The damage of unforgiveness has the power to affect generations and generations to come.

Unforgiveness creates a bondage that only limits the person that chooses to hold onto it. It puts you in a box and dares you to move beyond it. It dangles the wonderful world of possibilities in front of you but never really allows you to experience it.

Unforgiveness only lets you get but so far before it says, remember we hate that person, it says we don't smile because of what happen, we don't find the joy in things because we are always waiting for the next shoe to drop in life because of the endless cycle of let downs and lowered expectations which resulted from the bondage of unforgiveness.

Queen, it would be crazy to walk into a store and see a 40-year-old misbehaving and having a two-year old tantrum, right? Can you imagine her on the floor with her arms flaring all over the place, while she cries and pouts about not getting her way? It would be crazy right?

Unforgiveness Stops Growth

Unforgiveness has the same effect on you it stops your growth. While you have aged physically both mentally and spiritually you remain at the age when the offense took place. Yes, you have grown up but mentally you are still in that place of the rape, you are still in the place when your father left home, you are still in the place of being fired from your job. You are still in the place of being bullied, you are still in the place of _____ (you write it in). No matter how many years ago it happened, until you forgive, you will be stuck in that place. You can be so unbothered by bondage that you "forget" that it's there. It simply becomes a part of you.

How different would your life have been if this uninvited guest had never been there or allowed to stay? How different would your relationships have been? Would you have completed school? Would you still be married? Would you have kept the baby? Think for a moment just how different you would be right now if this uninvited guest had never been allowed to stay for so long.

In life someone (even those closest to us) will at some point offend you or hurt your feelings and, in most cases, never apologize for it. **Queen**, one cannot live life and never experience some level of pain, hurt, or offense, we cannot control the experience, but what you and I can control is our reaction to it. How do we respond when an offense takes place?

Maybe you need a moment to process the offense before you address it, maybe you have to address it right away, whatever the case, make sure you take a moment to address it. We simply were not meant to carry such offenses in our heart because they *drain, limit, and stop our growth.* Life is short enough as it is, why not live it without the hang ups of unforgiveness?

Tresniece Perry

Unforgiveness is a Choice

My daddy is my world. He is my go to for everything from wanting pizza delivered to my house (he lives in NY) to when some guy I was dating messes up. I talk to my daddy (yes even at 38 I still call him daddy) every week sometimes two or three times a week. My daddy can tell just by the sound of my voice when something is wrong. I am his number one fan (ok maybe I run a close tie with my sister) and he is mines.

If my daddy says it's going to be okay, guess what, it's going to be okay. I still look for my daddy to tell me that he is proud of me. I still want to make him proud of me. My daddy is my whole world. My daddy is my very own twin we are so much alike.

Yet, my daddy was my *greatest test of forgiveness.* The relationship I have with my daddy now has not always been the case. In being honest my daddy has always been my world just at one time that world was a little shattered.

I remember growing up and being so angry at my dad because he missed another important event. I remember being so sad that he was not around like my friends' dads were. I remember at different points in my life where I wanted him to be there more than he was capable of being in the moment. My dad had his own struggles he was dealing with but none of that mattered to me. All that mattered to me was he was not there when I needed him.

There was a point in my 20's where the anger and bitterness had gotten the best of me and I was officially done with my dad. While

I still loved him, I had reached a place where I had decided I no longer desired anything from him.

I remember two very distinctive moments in my life when God gave me the choice of forgiving my dad for not being there in the manner I desired. The first one came when I was in middle school I told this huge lie and got in trouble. When I got caught I used my daddy not being around as the reason for me seeking attention. My grandmother asked me, *"How long are you going to use that excuse to act the way you do?"*

The second moment would come later in my mid 20's. By this time, I was active in my church. I was in the choir. I was on the usher board. I was a youth leader and a minister in training but deep down inside I was still a little girl who wanted to be daddy's little girl. During this time God was starting His work on my dad. He was creating a change in him. God was answering the prayers of a 12-year-old little girl to restore her daddy and make him her daddy again. Due to my firm posture of unforgiveness I **REFUSED** see this and accept this answered prayer.

I was still choosing to hold onto the broken promises, missed birthdays and missed milestone moments because I felt I was justified in doing so. I felt like I earned the right to have these feelings. I felt like forgiving my dad was too easy. He needed to know what it felt like. He needed to understand how it felt to be a little girl and have people make fun of your dad.

There was a day, and I remember the details of the day but on this day, I was venting to God about my dad. In the middle of my venting session God asked, *"Do you know how different your life*

Tresniece Perry

would have been if I had allowed him to stay?" I remember just sitting there and while I had no response whatsoever I remember crying until my eyes hurt because I had never looked it at that way. I never looked at God removing my dad from my life as God's way of protecting me from my dad's lifestyle at the time.

Queen, this might be a hard thing to accept but there are times when God removes something or someone for our best interest. The removal protects the **PURPOSE** and **DESTINY** God placed on the inside of us. God will never place more on us than we can bear so in His protective way God simply removes the thing that will destroy us. God may decide to allow the thing or person to return or may He may not but ultimately, it's His choice.

In that moment I made the choice to forgive. I made the choice to let go of every hurt, missed moment, or what I saw as failure on my dad's part. I made the choice to fully embrace my dad, his past, his present, and his future. I made the choice to simply love him unconditionally.

This was a process and I stumbled along the way. *Queen*, I didn't always get it right. There was this time not too long after I had decided to forgive my dad where the forgiveness was tested. It was something as simple as my dad asking me to drive my car to the store.

My response was yes but don't treat it like you do your cars. He just looked at me and got out the car. He didn't take my car and I remember feeling bad because once again I brought up his past. It's as if I could not let him forget something he lived. *Queen* God checked me and told me that I needed to get past it and truly let it go.

Forgiveness is about letting go of everything even the smallest detail. God needed me to understand that if I was to truly forgive my dad then I needed to be able to see past his mistakes. They were not something that I could keep bringing up. The same if for you **Queen**, when you make the choice to forgive understand you're forgetting everything attached to the offense. You are making the choice to move forward from it and not bring it back up again.

Forgiveness is for You

Once I decided to forgive God was able to come in and restore me and my daddy's relationship. The relationship I spoke of earlier is a direct result of me being willing to let it all go. To simply move past it. To not allow it to continue to have a hold over my life or my relationship.

The thing that never occurred to me even as an adult was the unforgiveness was only hurting me. My daddy like the person who offended you was still living their life. Your offender went on to graduate high school. Get married or remarried, had more kids, get the dream job, moved into a new house, bought a new car and went on to be successful or maybe they didn't the point is their lives kept going forward and your life stood still. The moment you made the choice to hold onto unforgiveness, you made the choice to stand still. Life is passing you by and you are stuck in by choice.

Tresniece Perry

The Impact of Unforgiveness

Colossians 3:12-14

So, as God's own chosen people, who are holy [set apart, sanctified for His purpose] and well-beloved [by God Himself], put on a heart of compassion, kindness, humility, gentleness, and patience [which has the power to endure whatever injustice or unpleasantness comes, with good temper]; [13] bearing graciously with one another, and willingly forgiving each other if one has a cause for complaint against another; just as the Lord has forgiven you, so should you forgive. [14] Beyond all these things put on and wrap yourselves in [unselfish] love, which is the perfect bond of unity [for everything is bound together in agreement when each one seeks the best for others].

Amplified Bible (AMP)

My inability to forgive was causing my monthly cycles to be unbearable. It was having a direct impact on my dating life. It was causing me to side eye God. How did God expect me to look at him as my "father" when my father here on earth was not doing right? I was angry and didn't know why. It opened me up to experience and bask in rejection as if it was a badge of honor to be displayed.

Queen, there is a direct relationship between the relationship with your father and every man you meet. If there is unforgiveness in your heart concerning your natural father there will be this unspoken wall up between you and God. How long will you hold God, your husband and your sons' hostage for the sins of your natural father?

Queen stop holding them hostage to your past. You kept asking God to come in, but you will only let him but so far because in your eyes God cannot be trusted. You equate the love (or lack thereof) of your natural father to God. You have a hard time releasing to God your most private thoughts (yes, He already knows them, but He would love for you to share them with Him) or moments to God because you are unsure if He will be there to catch you. You are SPECIAL to God and He desires nothing more than to have a *relationship with you.* Know that religion and relationship are two different things.

God wants to spend time with you getting to know you and you getting to know Him. Learn of Him and His ways beyond what you hear on Sunday or at Bible Study. God wants your relationship with Him to be so personal that even amid a storm you can still hear His voice and move with Him.

Queen, not every story will end like me and my daddy's. God gave me time to build this new relationship with my daddy. For some of you that moment has passed. For whatever reason the person who created the offense is no longer available for you speak to. That's okay because again this is about you and not them.

I must ask the question are you ready to forgive? Take a moment and really think about it. Are you really ready to move past the place that has cost you more than you know?

Forgiveness is Not Friendship

Forgiving does not mean you have to be best friends with the person who created the offense. It does not mean that you even have to engage them in activity. *Forgiving does not equal friendship.* People will tell you that you have allow the offender back into your life, but you don't. You do not have to have any type of relationship with the offender after you forgive.

Forgiving is about your release, your ability to move forward and become the woman God called you to be. The type of forgiveness God desires is the removal of even the residue of the offense from our memory. Gods desire for you is to be so unaffected by the offense not even the sight of the offender, not a song or movie, not their name or any other attachment to them can cause you to stumble and fall.

Queen, *the opposite of unforgiveness is love.* When you love someone, I mean really love someone you can see past their faults and love them anyway. You can love them the way God loves you; unconditionally.

First Corinthians 13:4-5
⁴ Love endures with patience and serenity, love is kind and thoughtful, and is not jealous or envious; love does not brag and is not proud or arrogant. ⁵ It is not rude; it is not self-seeking, it is not provoked [nor overly sensitive and easily angered]; it does not take into account a wrong endured.
Amplified Bible (AMP)

This is a necessary process for you to move forward in your life. It is required if you really want to "Fix Your Crown".

The three R's of the forgiving process:

1. **Repent:** Ask God to forgive you for holding onto the unforgiveness, even if you feel justified in holding onto it, it is not right. Asking God for forgives of holding the offense captive opens the door for God to forgive you of your sins.

2. **Release:** Get a piece of paper and write a letter. Write a letter to your offender (relax you are NOT going to mail it). In this letter explain the offense and its impact on your life. Be as honest as you need to be in this letter. Release every emotion or feeling you have tied to this offense. At the end of the letter tell the offender I forgive you (only write it if you really mean it). Give that letter to God and ask Him to remove not only the offense but everything attached to it. The letter itself can go in the trash.

3. **Restore:** Ask God to restore you. Ask God to go in and do surgery on your mind so that every thought attached to offense He will remove. God promises in His word:

Isaiah 61:3-4
To grant to those who mourn in Zion the following: To give them a [a]turban instead of dust [on their heads, a sign of mourning], The oil of joy instead of mourning, The garment [expressive] of praise instead of a disheartened spirit.
Amplified Bible (AMP)

Queen, God promised that He will give you these things in place of what you lost. If you allow God to take you on this journey of forgiveness God will make it so your heart show no signs of the damage that was created.

Tresniece Perry

God will completely restore your ability to give and receive love. Letting go of unforgiveness is a process that may take longer than one day. God may have to take through this process in layers. Don't focus on how long this process is for God is not looking for a quick fix but a permeant one. Allow God to deal with this so that you can fix your crown and step on.

Once this process is complete God will tackle your victim mindset. The mindset that tells you, you are entitled to act and feel like a victim. This mindset will make excuses for your behavior instead of owning your behavior. It will tell you that everything that goes wrong in life is not your fault. God is now looking to address your victim mindset.

The Victim Mindset

Victim: one that is acted on and usually adversely affected by a force or agent; a person harmed, injured, or killed because of a crime, accident, or other event or action

Overcomer: a person who overcomes something: one who succeeds in dealing with or gaining control of some problem or difficulty

Romans 5:3-5
3-5 There's more to come: We continue to shout our praise even when we're hemmed in with troubles, because we know how troubles can develop passionate patience in us, and how that patience in turn forges the tempered steel of virtue, keeping us alert for whatever God will do next. In alert expectancy such as this, we're never left feeling shortchanged. Quite the contrary—we can't round up enough containers to hold everything God generously pours into our lives through the Holy Spirit!
The Message (MSG)

Tresniece Perry

$\mathscr{I}$ remember one Sunday after a powerful alter call, I was getting up off the floor and one of the other ministers said to me, "When you truly want to be free you will be." Immediately the ego side of me took offense. I mean clearly since I was getting off the floor after going to the alter I wanted to be free. I remember looking her and thinking she is crazy while I fixed my makeup. No matter how hard I tried to shake her words I simply could not.

Her question made me think, was I really free or was I simply going through the motions of being free. You know what I mean, the motion of waving my hands at the right time at church to being overly dramatic during praise and worship. Doing all the things one would do when they want to look and sound free.

It would be a few weeks later when God would ask me the exact same question and my answer would be Lord who does not really want to be free. God said in response "this means letting go of playing the victim". What God was asking me was are you ready to stop using the valley moments in life to justify the way I was acting or my refusal to be obedient to God's word.

The question caused me to pause because when I thought about it being the "victim" had gotten me far. It got me sympathy when needed, it excused more bad judgments and mistakes, it okayed my sense of everybody owing me something and finally it justified my sense of entitlement.

Queen, I was content in living the rest of my life with this victim mentality. Never truly embracing God had granted me access to a life of freedom. Instead I chose to be content living my life inside the cell of a victim even with the cell unlocked and opened.

In the last chapter we dealt with forgiveness this chapter God wants us to deal with the mindset of a victim. Note after an offense and depending on the offense, the offense can have lasting influence over our life. The offense can shape how we chose to deal with people. It can shape the type of job that we take, the person we date and maybe even marry. This offense has the power to shape our views on the world and things attached to it. The biggest thing is that it has the power to shape our relationship and interaction with God.

Remember the offense you were to release in the former chapter. Not the surface offense like your coworker didn't speak to you this morning or someone cut you off in traffic. No, I am speaking about the offense that altered your view of God. The offense that caused you to question God's place in your life. You know the offense that was life shifting and changing. The offense that even to this day, people know the impact it had on your life.

Now the good news is that you have come out of the other side of this offense, but the sad part is that your mind is still there. While you have moved forward physically mentally you are still in the place of the offense and now it has made you a victim. Now there is a sense of people owing you something. A sense of entitlement because you went through what you went through.

There is a sense that people are supposed to forgive your bad attitude because you went through that. People are supposed to overlook your overly dramatic ways because this thing happened to you. People are supposed to take care of you and make sure that you

Tresniece Perry

are ok because this awful thing happened to you. The crazy part is this thing happened a long time ago. It's not a recent offense. This offense happened some 5, 10, 15 or even 20 years; yet you are still using it to justify your behavior.

Still A Victim

There was a quadriplegic man in the bible. The name of this man was not given he was simply known by the condition that made him a victim. This man lived in an area where once a year an angel would come down to a certain pool and touch it giving the water healing powers. This process would not last long and you have to be quick to get into the water. All the people needed a healing knew when this time was coming, and they made their way to the pool.

So, the man was competing against others who had their own stories and their own reason for being there. He was competing with those who could get up by themselves, walk or run. It seemed unfair. Almost as if he was at a disadvantage because of his condition.

For 38 years this man went to the pool area but never made it in. Now maybe after the first or second year he said, "I will get there next year," but by year 38 his mindset had changed. He was no longer trying to make it to the water.

His mindset was someone should be helping him to the water. He started to look at the people who got healed with the side eye. His condition had not affected his body but now it shaped his mindset as well. One day this man encounters Jesus at this pool and Jesus asked him, "Do you want to made whole?" To the Jesus the man replies, "Sir I have no one to put me in." **(John 5:1-15)**

Now you are thinking, how crazy is that? Here this man is with Jesus and Jesus is asking him if he wants to be whole and the first thing the man says is sir there is no one to put me in the water. That's a victim mindset. Now we can go with the argument that maybe, just maybe, he didn't know who Jesus was. Maybe he was shocked at the question that was asked of him.

Maybe he thought it was a trick question or maybe he looked down at himself and thought that was a dumb question. Whatever the reason he didn't just say yes to the question. His reply was not a loud resounding "Yes, I want to be healed".

Is this what he had been waiting for? For someone to "help" get what he wanted. For someone, anyone to take just a moment and see him? But when Jesus saw him his victim mindset stopped him from moving forward.

Now before you judge this man be honest how many times has God asked you if you wanted to be whole and your response was, "But you don't know what they did to me." Maybe you responded, "But God you should have been there." Maybe your response was, "But I gave him everything and it still wasn't enough." Maybe you said, "I will forgive but I will never forget." All these excuses help to keep you in the mindset of a victim. The mindset of a victim tells you that no matter how much you try, nothing is going to work out for you. That you will never get past it. That the offense will forever be a part of your life.

The mindset of a victim *limits your ability to trust and believe in God* and His promises. The mindset of a victim tells you that everyone has to pay for their mistakes. The mindset of a victim tells you that you are entitled to be mean and hateful. The mindset of victim tells you that you now have the right to make others feel the pain and hurt you feel.

The mindset of a victim will have you believing that even God should bend to your irrational thoughts and actions. The mindset of a victim will make way for you to create additional victims. Broken people break other people. If you operate in the mindset of a victim everything you build will be broken. Nothing can sustain a broken foundation.

While writing this I was made aware of my entitled feelings towards God. I felt like I was entitled to God doing what I wanted him to do, when I wanted him to do it because I grew up without my dad being physically in my life.

Deep down in my heart I felt like God owed me that. God owed me the right to have everything in my adult life be perfect. God was supposed to make sure I lacked for nothing and everything I was waiting on should have been right there. No, I should not have to wait because my childhood was hard, my adult life should be a piece of cake.

Sound crazy huh? Yet, with my saved and Holy Ghost filled self, this is where my deepest thoughts went. Now I would never voice this opinion to anyone. I would never tell anyone what I was thinking or share this. I felt when God didn't let something happen for me that happened for others, that He was being unfair. I felt that God had favorites and I was not one of the (even though I am His favorite, we all are). On that beautiful morning like a ton of bricks I realized how entitled I felt and how it was shaping my daily life.

Girl Fix Your Crown

See *Queen,* the role of a victim had been part of my life for so long just like the man mentioned above, my thoughts were impacted by it. A victim is always looking for someone to do for them what only God can do. A person operating in the mindset of a victim will destroy relationships because the person will not bend to their need. A mindset of a victim will stop God from being able grant freedom.

Just like anything we do in life the longer we do it the more normal it becomes. Acting in the role of being a victim can become your new normal *Queen,* unless you take the proper steps change it. There is a cycle that a victim moves in.

Cycle of the Victim Mindset:

1. **Pity:** a victim wants anyone listening to their story to feel sorry for them. Their actions require those who listen to feel a certain way about them. Examples of this: acting real extra to gain sympathy or posting certain things on social media to gain attention.

2. **Manipulation:** when the pity stops working, the victim will result to using this tactic to get the person that's listening to bend to their wishes by saying stuff like, "I am trying to do better but it's just so hard now".

3. **Anger:** when neither the pity or manipulation is working, finally they will result to anger to get their way. They will throw tantrums, stop speaking to you and curse you out, all to get you to bow to their wishes.

This cycle will continue repeatedly until the victim decides to change it. Some victims will spend their entire life being a victim. Sound familiar? Do you know someone like this? *Queen* are you like this? This cycle does damage as it stops God from being able to deliver you fully from things in your past. Taking this posture or this *mindset limits how far you will go in life.* How can God use you to change the world when you still want to be in the cell your offense created?

What you went through was part of your story but not the entire story. Gods intent was to use the offense to push you into the **PURPOSE** and **PLAN** He had for your life. Understand this, nothing that happens to us takes God by surprise. God is an intentional God so everything that happens is working in your favor.

James 1:2-4

Consider it nothing but joy, my brothers and sisters, whenever you fall into various trials. ³ Be assured that the testing of your faith [through experience] produces endurance [leading to spiritual maturity, and inner peace]. ⁴ And let endurance have its perfect result and do a thorough work, so that you may be perfect and completely developed [in your faith], lacking in nothing.
Amplified Bible (AMP)

That's right *Queen*, it all is working out something on the inside of you. I know this way of thinking can be hard to embrace but to move forward you must. Your ability to overcome this victim mindset is directly linked to you obtaining every promise God as for you.

There is a **PURPOSE** in the testing and trails you have been through. All of it is working the gift God placed inside of you. Many people found their way to Jesus because of the trails they were facing in life. Trails have a way of bringing even the strongest person to their knees, but it is worth it.

Romans 8:28
And we know [with great confidence] that God [who is deeply concerned about us] causes all things to work together [as a plan] for good for those who love God, to those who are called according to His plan and purpose.
Amplified Bible (AMP)

Understand your trail was created, designed, and put in place especially for you. While others may experience a similar trial, your trials will differ. The reason is what God is birthing on the inside of you doesn't match what He is birthing on the inside of them. Every tear has a **PURPOSE!** Every pain has a **PURPOSE!** Every challenging moment has a **PURPOSE!**

The issue becomes when dealing with various trials, setbacks, disappointments we tend to hold onto the issue and simply stop moving. We embrace each of these things and make them the reason we stop going to church, praying, and growing. We use these items as a reason to push God away and become a victim of the issue.

As long you chose to be a victim you will be. **Queen,** not taking away from what you have been through nor the steps you have made to be better. My question to you now **Queen** is, do you want to be a victim to it for the rest of your life?
Freedom

Queen, when I think of the word freedom, it can seem a little unreal, almost like it's impossible. **Queen** I mean can we truly live in freedom? Free from past hurts, failures, pain, free from rejection and its residue, free from anger and hate, free from sadness, free from the need to please others, free from the bondage of self-doubt, etc.??? Is this a real possibility? Is it really possible to live in this world and experience the freedom that we have shouted about on Sunday mornings?

The answer to these questions is YES! Yes, *Queen* it is very possible to live a life of total and complete freedom. You can have a life where the past is not shaping your present thoughts and actions. *Queen* your life can be lived in such a way that you don't walk in the fear of being rejected. *Queen* your present life can be such that your past hurts and pains don't determine the quality of your relationships today. *Queen* your actions with people can be actions from the heart and not because you are afraid they will not love just you.

Queen with God as the center of your life. Freedom is not only a possibility it's a reality. Anyplace where God is allowed to be God there can be freedom. Meaning *Queen,* you have to wait to be free in an area and then allow God permission to come in and remove all the attachments to the offense.

John 8:36
So, if the Son sets you free from sin, then become a true son
and be unquestionably free!
The Passion Translation (TPT)

Freedom is a choice. **Queen** before we can even start to talk about any level of true freedom the first question is *Queen* do you want to be free. *Queen* you have to decide if freedom is what you want. Then you will stop playing the role of victim. You will stop giving into the emotions of failure, loneliness, etc. You shift your thinking to embrace what God says about you and stop waiting for man to approve you.

Freedom is a choice first and an action second. **Queen** your actions have to show you are free!! No more settling for being the runner up you are worth more than that!! Girl stop allowing your body to be used nothing more than a release for your frustrations and realize your body is a temple. Stop treating it with such disregard.

Queen understand how powerful your body is. For out of your body comes the gift of life. God created your body in such a way it has the ability to carry and birth life. Stop allowing it to be violated by people who don't understand it's value (and that includes you).

Queen no more playing the victim now you own the role of VICTOR!! Your actions have to be followed by staying in the word of God. God's word is what will change you from the inside out. **Queen** fix your crown and release the mindset of the victim.

Now that you have released the victim mindset it's time for you to embrace a new way of thinking. It's time for you to think and act like the **Queen** you are. It's time for you to embrace your **Queen** mindset.

A Queen's Mindset

Thoughts: something that is thought: such as:

a: an individual act or product of thinking

b: a developed intention or plan had no thought of leaving home

c: something (such as an opinion or belief) in the mind he spoke his thoughts freely

d: the intellectual product or the organized views and principles of a period, place, group, or individual contemporary Western thought

Romans 12:2

Stop imitating the ideals and opinions of the culture around you but be inwardly transformed by the Holy Spirit through a total reformation of how you think. This will empower you to discern God's will as you live a beautiful life, satisfying and perfect in his eyes.

The Passion Translation (TPT)

You're too fat; you're not smart enough; you're a failure; you're ugly; you stutter you're a disappointment...

These are just some of the thoughts that I use to believe about myself before I started my relationship with God.

Girl Fix Your Crown

You're not as anointed as Rev. So, and So, You're too young; God loves you but He doesn't like you; No one will listen; you've made too many mistakes; God has favorites and you're not it; you will always be broke; that's just how I am.

These are some of the thoughts I had after I truly started my relationship with God.

The common thread with these thoughts were each one was

lie. None of them represented what God thought of me or how God wanted me to think about myself. There was a lie that was told to me, I accepted as my truth thus watering my "perceived" thoughts about God. These thoughts then turned into my "reason" for living how I was living. My excuse not give my all or trust God and His plan for my life.

Queen, *your thoughts have POWER!* What you think, you speak thus what you will become. Your thoughts become your words thus leading to your actions. This is why it is so important to do as Philippians 4:8 says:

Finally, [a]believers, whatever is true, whatever is honorable and worthy of respect, whatever is right and confirmed by God's word, whatever is pure and wholesome, whatever is lovely and brings peace, whatever is admirable and of good repute; if there is any excellence, if there is anything worthy of praise, think continually on these things [center your mind on them, and implant them in your heart].
Amplified Bible (AMP)

Tresniece Perry

Just for a moment think about how many thoughts go through your mind every day? How many times your brain wonders away from the actual task. How many times your thoughts cause you to miss something God is trying to get you to see?

All of the thoughts that enter your mind throughout the day, do 1 or 2 things:

1. Hinders your destiny
2. *Enables your destiny*

When starting this chapter, I shared some thoughts I battled with at different stages through my life. Each negative thought battled against the Word of God. A thought is the opinion of someone (even yourself) that you accepted to be true. A flower will never grow unless it is first planted and takes root. Thoughts are the same way.

A thought first must be planted on the inside of you and then you have to water it in order for it to grow. **Queen**, when it comes to your thoughts the question is do your thoughts match those of Gods thoughts about you?

When we enter into the world we are blank slate. Our experiences, encounters with people, our upbringing, and people's opinions of us shape who we become. Your thoughts reflect all the things mentioned above. Stop accepting the lies of the devil to be true for your life.

When we read the Word of God it tells us we are fearfully and wonderfully made but if my thoughts tell me I am ugly, I am fat or too skinny then who do I believe? God says you are the lender not the borrower, but your thoughts tell you no matter what you will always be broke. The moment you decide to believe and act on these negative thoughts you effectively cancel out the very promise God gave you.

There is a cycle to your life. A cycle which sets the tone for how you respond to God. How you interpret His thoughts and promises concerning you. This cycle either hinders or helps you to embrace the Word of God in your life and what's spoken over your life.

The thought cycle governs so much of your life. Yet are often times over looked and undervalued. The devil knows the impact of your thoughts. He understands as long as he is able to get a footing in your mind he is in the prime position to cause you to stumble, fall, forfeit or cancel out the *PROMISES, PLANS, PURPOSE and DESTINY* God has you marked for. The **"Thought Process"** is four steps:

1. **Thought Given:** it normally comes from an opinion either someone feeds you or you create on your own about yourself and/or God. It can also be shaped by an experience good or bad.

2. **Thought Accepted:** you have to accept it as truth before it will manifest in your brain. Once accepted it is hard to undo the thought especially if its attached to a traumatic experience or memory.

3. **Thought Spoken:** you confess the truth making it more real. An example would be you saying, "I knew this would happen...nothing works in my favor". Now that you have spoken you start to expect the negativity to always find you.

4. **Thought Acted Out:** you stop trying to see God's hand over your life. You are always waiting for the "other shoe to drop". You act out the negativity. You walk through life with the expectation God will let you down.

Each step carries its own actions and has its own consequences attached to it. However; each step is needed to move forward. Even when it comes to good thoughts *Queen* you have to first be willing to accept the good stuff.

I once heard someone say it's easier to believe the bad stuff than the good stuff. *Queen* we can justify all day why we believe the negative stuff, but for God to change our thinking we must be willing. *Queen*, you don't have to accept a thought just because it popped up in your brain. When a negative thought comes you have the **POWER** of your words to cancel out the thought.

There are underlining thoughts God needs to deal with because they have kept you stagnate. They stop you from growing and reaching your **PURPOSE.** These thoughts have shaped your past and your present, but God says it won't shape your future. These thoughts block you from seeing, acting and moving as the *Queen* God created you to be. God must uproot and destroy these thoughts as they are setting the tone of your relationship with Him. Your thoughts matter! This is why in Romans 12: 2 it tells you to renew your mind because God knew long before we act on anything, reject him and His Word, it first starts in the mind.

It was this way with Jeremiah, Moses, Abraham, and Sarah. There were some thoughts which had settled down in the core of who they were to such a degree that even when God himself was talking to them or in their presence they couldn't receive it.

In the Bible we encounter Jeremiah **(Jeremiah 1:4-10)** speaking with God who just told him he was prophet to the nation's. The angle tells Jeremiah in His mother's womb he was crafted, created, and purposed for this work yet his response was I am only a child. Since when did age factor into God's plan for our life? Jeremiah needed to check his thought life. I wonder what shaped that thought in Jeremiah? I wonder who told him because of his age he was not useful. I wonder who told him to stay in a child's place. I wonder when Jeremiah made the choice to believe them?

Queen, I wonder who pointed out Moses' **(Exodus 4:10-11)** speech impediment? The Moses we encounter in this portion of scripture and the chapter before is a different Moses then we hear about earlier in the bible. This Moses has been through a few things and as a result his thoughts about himself have shifted. The thoughts of himself have shifted to such a degree that even when he is talking to God the negativity and all of the reasons why God can't use him come to light.

Moses thoughts about himself were so bad he was willing to talk himself out of the **PURPOSE AND PLAN** God had created for his life. Through the mistakes and failures Moses had made, Moses had become content to be in the background. He had learned to be quiet and to blend in. I wonder who told him to be silent or laughed when he spoke?

The problem with that is God's plan for Moses life put him right in the front. God never created Moses to be in the background. From

Tresniece Perry

the moment of his birth God had marked Moses for greatness. Everything in his life pointed to that even when he couldn't see it.

This is the same is for you. God never intended you to be a background player in your own life. From the moment of your conception (prior to you even being born) God marked you for greatness. I don't want to be the one to break this news to you but no matter how much you try to blend God will make you stand out. God decided you would be **GREAT** and whether you achieve this kicking and screaming or by walking in His **PURPOSE**, will come to past.

God's plan included Moses' mistakes too, they *qualified his service* for God. **Queen** you spend so much time trying to hide the mistakes you have made not knowing those very mistakes make you usable to God. When God picked his 12 disciples they were made up of fisherman, a tax collector, a thief, a zealot (a rebel) and more.

In other words, Jesus did not go and get the people who knew the scriptures or who lived perfect lives. *He needed/wanted flawed people to reach a flawed world that would lead to a Perfect Savior.* This is why God wanted Moses, yet all Moses could think about was how unqualified he was. His thoughts were impacting his future. His thoughts were in danger of talking himself out of the plan God had for him.

Queen we don't come out thinking we look different or talk different it is a learned behavior. We aren't born thinking our head is too big or ears too small for our body. We are not born with the thoughts of failure or disappointment. We are not born with the thought of not being good enough or never measuring up. No, these thoughts and ones like it become part of our thought processing as we go through life. Someone points something out and we focus on it. Someone plants a negative thought and latch onto for dear life. The thought becomes so true we settle it to be real even if God says different.

Thoughts and Your Words

Matthew 15:11
It is not what goes into the mouth of a man that defiles and dishonors him, but what comes out of the mouth, this defiles and dishonors him.
Amplified Bible (AMP)

Queens we have the power to talk ourselves right out the very blessing God promised because our thought life is out sorts. What you think you will become. The reason is simple if thinking it long enough you will start to believe, once you start to believe it you start to speak it and finally when you start speaking it you start to act in (walk in it). You believe you are stupid, so you stopped trying when you were in school or even now on your job.

You believe you were unworthy of real love, so you settled for the guy who wasn't *equipped, purposed, or even chosen to love you the right way.* Thus, making him ill equipped to handle the **PURPOSE** and **DESTINY** God hand crafted for you. Now *Queen* understand this does not make him a bad person he's just wrong for you. The more you try to make him into something he was never created to be the more you set yourself up for disappointment and heartache (different chapter in the book).

You believed you were cursed so when God sends you His blessing you reject it, or half way enjoy because you are "waiting for the other shoe to drop". You speak, breath, and live in a negative space secretly hoping something good will come but expecting the worst. *Queen*, how do you pray for God's best but expect the devils worst and yet when things don't go in your favor blame God? Truth: *you are your WORDS!*

Proverbs 18:21
Death and life are in the power of the tongue,
And those who love it and indulge it will eat its fruit and bear
the consequences of their words.
Amplified Bible (AMP)

Stop speaking death into your life *Queen*. Stop speaking it to and over your kids. Speaking things like "you are just like your no-good father" or "you will never be anything." Stop calling your children dumb, lazy, trifling, etc. Stop telling your husband he no good or he is a horrible husband. Even if currently all of these things are true, you are required to speak life over them. *Queen* you cancel out the altar call prayer, the prayer group meeting, and even Sunday morning service when you speak negative. You are creating a death sentence for your situation and all those attached to it.

Changed Thinking

Understand my thoughts didn't change at the snap of a finger when I got saved. If anything, my negative thoughts become more intense. Now there was a battle happening in my mind between all the lies the enemy had ever told me, what I believed to be true, finally what I accepted vs. what God said I was. I had to make the choice to believe the truth over the lie. *Queen* you do have a say in the matter. As I mentioned in a different chapter God is a gentleman, so He allows you the opportunity to choose. Recognize each option has its own set of reactions.

Queen you must *retrain your mind and your thoughts.* The thought about you being a failure has dictated your life from the moment you accepted it. It directed how well you did in school. What jobs you applied for. The men you dated and for some - the man you married. It directed how you raised your kids especially your daughters.

That one thought has been with you for what seems like forever, but you have to denounce the thought, pray God removes it and finally start to retrain your mind cancel it out when it tries to return.

You must shape your thoughts in a way that mirror the very image of God and His thoughts concerning you. Your thoughts must reflect what the Word of God says you are. God will force you to go to those thoughts and the root cause. Freedom is only good when it shifts the way you think, when it shifts how you live, when it shifts your life.

The freedom mentioned in this book needs to be deep on the inside of you, as it births a change in the generations that come after you. A freedom that shifts your life into the next level of abundance. This new freedom will change the bloodline and redetermine destiny.

Counter Measures:

Hebrews 4:12-13
God means what he says. What he says goes. His powerful
Word is sharp as a surgeon's scalpel, cutting through
everything, whether doubt or defense, laying us open to listen
and obey. Nothing and no one is impervious to God's Word.
We can't get away from it—no matter what. The Message
(MSG)

The **WORD OF GOD** is your first counter measure when it comes to retraining your mind *Queen*. Even with all the power the Word has, it's only as powerful to the degree in which you know it and apply it. It's the **WORD** that causes things in the natural to line up with the spiritual. The **WORD** causes sickness to leave your body and reminds us God is the creator of all things. The **WORD** is what tells you God has accepted you, flaws and all. Therefore, it's key to retraining your thoughts.

Romans 10:8
But what does it say? "The word is near you, in your mouth
and in your heart"—that is, the word [the message, the basis]
of faith which we preach.
Amplified Bible (AMP)

The **WORD** has the power to go to the root of the thought (the place where the thought was created) and destroy it. If you kill and remove the root and the leaves and branch will die and fall off. The root is what God is after.

Written Reminders

Queen for every negative thought you encounter, ask God to give you an encouraging word or scripture. Maybe it's a positive saying that speaks to you. Whatever it is write it down and post it on your mirror, in your journal, in your car or wherever you need a reminder.

In the same manner our military spends time studying and preparing for the enemy to attack, you have to be the same way. Stay on guard! Your mind is a battlefield, but you have already been destined to **WIN** you just have to be *willing to fight.*

1 Peter 5:8-9
⁸ Be sober [well balanced and self-disciplined], be alert and cautious at all times. That enemy of yours, the devil, prowls around like a roaring lion [fiercely hungry], seeking someone to devour. ⁹ But resist him, be firm in your faith [against his attack—rooted, established, immovable]. Amplified Bible (AMP)

The devil is counting on you not being free. Having a *Queen* mindset is important because there are others depending on your freedom, so you can go back and help them get theirs. There are lives hanging in the balance and their freedom depends on you.

You never letting go of the way your parents treated you or you never releasing the divorce or the abortion, all creates a path for bondage and until you release that stuff mentality everything you touch has a *residue of bondage attached* to it. That is why some of the things you are asking, praying, fasting for and laying claim to, God can't release because right now, if you got it you would taint it.

It's time to have the mindset of a *Queen* - are you READY! Once you reach the place where your thoughts match that of a *Queen* you are now ready to shift your reality to a faith-based reality.

Faith Based Reality

Faith: a. (1) belief and trust in and loyalty to God (2): belief in the traditional doctrines of a religion

b. (1): firm belief in something for which there is no proof

(2): complete trust

(3): something that is believed especially with strong conviction

Reality: a. (1) the quality or state of being real

(2) a real event, entity, or state of affairs

b. (1) the totality of real things and events

(2) something that is neither derivative nor dependent but exists necessarily

Habakkuk 2:3
And then God answered: "Write this. Write what you see. Write it out in big block letters so that it can be read on the run. This vision-message is a witness pointing to what's coming. It aches for the coming—it can hardly wait! And it doesn't lie. If it seems slow in coming, wait. It's on its way. It will come right on time.
The Message (MSG)

Tresniece Perry

*H*ow many times have you made this statement?

"This is just how I am" or the statement *"I will always be broke,"* or *"He will never change."* These statements and those like them serve no purpose but to keep your stuck in your present reality. Your present reality is what shapes your present thought life.

There is a strong misconception when a person gets saved every problem in their life goes away. Some even believe nothing bad should ever happen to Christians because they serve God and He would not let anything come up against His people. This simply is not true. If anyone was to spend real time with a believer, they would know things still happen. Loved ones still pass, unexpected bills still show up, people leave, marriages come to an end, people lose jobs, homes, and cars - in other words believers' *faith in God does get tested.*

Queen, you must be willing to adjust how you see things. Asking yourself how do you see and interpret the pieces of your life? Applying faith to your reality does not mean nothing bad will happen it just means when things start to get shaky, you turn to God who is your source.

In Proverbs 4:23 it tells us *"above all else, guard your heart, for everything you do flows from it."* The matters of the heart are the very things that will bring any person down to their knees. It's the place where love dwells. It's the place where total completeness dwells. Understanding this connection is vital because there is a direct connection between the matters of your heart and your ability to apply faith to your reality. When your heart is tainted, broken, damaged, or even bruised it will be hard (not impossible) for you to apply any measure of faith to your reality.

Queen your present reality does not determine your future, your faith does. *Your faith determines your future.* Your ability to apply faith to your reality is truly a life and death matter. Your reality is shaped by the present things you see only because you have not been given the insight to your future. Presently your reality may tell you to reject the possibility of anything getting better in your life. You can even pull up "evidence" to support your claims or the justifications for your trust in your own reality vs trusting a faith-based reality.

The problem with your reality is that it:

1. Leaves no place for God
2. Leaves no place for your faith to work
3. Has a bad outcome

When you tap into a faith-based reality just the opposite:

1. You allow God to work
2. Your faith opens the doors for God to move
3. It provides the path to your happy ending

Matthew 17:20

He answered, "Because of your little faith [your lack of trust and confidence in the power of God]; for I assure you and most solemnly say to you, [a]if you have [living] faith the size of a mustard seed, you will say to this mountain, 'Move from here

Tresniece Perry

to there,' and [if it is God's will] it will move; and nothing will be impossible for you.
Amplified Bible (AMP)

Faith is an active action. It's something you have to actively apply to your reality, daily, hour by hour, minute by minute and sometimes depending on the day, second by second. Your faith action does not have to be something you post on social media or even something that you tell your good girlfriend. Your faith action can be as simple as you are reading a scripture in the bible or refusing to accept failure or defeat as an option in any area of your life.

There are countless stories in the Bible where Jesus healed someone because of their faith. They took their faith and made it action and caused Jesus to respond. Faith makes you *disregard your reality and embrace a faith-based reality.* A faith-based reality blocks out the naysayers, faith-based reality rebukes and cancels out negative thoughts from taking root. Faith-based reality knows and understands that within yourself you are not able to overcome but with God you will **WIN** in every area.

Taking God at His Word means speaking the **WORD** even when things in your current reality don't line up to the Word. It's refusing to surrender to your problems. Faith gives you the power to see yourself as a *Queen*.

Queen, your faith will encourage you to know God is in your corner and handling the devils that are trying to take you out. God can change, adjust or shift anything you face in your favor. All God requires you to do is believe He can do it. *Queen*, the key to living this **Queen** life is shifting your reality. Understanding your life, the flow of your life is under the direction of God.

Faith Based Vision

One of the hardest lessons to understand is, not everyone will understand or accept the vision God has given you concerning your life. Stop expecting those around you to get with or agree with your vision. You must *be SECURE* in the vision of God and the Word of God for your reality. Your posture must be even if your circle is looking at you with one eye you trust the Word and God.

Queen you can't stop because uncle so and so doubts you. If, your parents are not supporting you, keep going. If family members are laughing and talking about you, keep going. Keep going knowing God gave you the vision, which means *He has equipped you to carry it* and complete it. You can't expect those who do not know the vision to support the process of the vision.

Case in point: One of my other gifts is that I am a makeup artist. I use various social media platforms to post my work. Now my work could be me doing my face for the day or one of my clients. I have booked many clients simply off the work that I posted.

There was this one time I posted a picture on one of MY social media pages. I really don't remember what the picture was. A family member commented on the picture saying that it was too much and then went on to say I posted too much and added some other opinions of me that had no merit.

At first it bothered me and had me questioning, wow was I really posting too much. Did I come off as being self-absorbed? I mean, was I really offending people by my posting? It got so bad that I stopped posting every day. Sometimes I would post every other week or once a week. Then I felt like I needed to explain the reason for the post.

One day it just clicked...God reminded me that my posting opened doors for my business. A good portion of my business last year came from referrals and social media posting. For every person who would tell me you are posting too much, someone else would say I love logging on and seeing your post. That's it right there this makeup vision was given to me by God, so it was foolish of me to allow the opinions of someone else to deter the vision.

Working my business under the guidelines of God, it was not my job to fit into the role of someone else. The vision was not theirs, so they could not understand the vision process. For every vision there is a process God has outlined for the vision. You must trust that process and not the people around you.

In the book of Genesis there is a story about a man who God gave a vision and word to. When God gave this vision, it didn't match the present reality this man found himself in. Despite what it looked like this man embraced, obeyed, and did what God told him to do. He didn't stop when people looked at him funny while they walked by. He didn't stop when people started to talk about him. He didn't stop when those around him asked him if he was crazy. See, all this man knew was God gave him the vision...not his neighbors, not his friends or family members.

God trusted him enough with the vision. **Queen** understand when God places a vision in you that means He is trusting you with it. You were personally selected for this vision. God could have given it to the person who on paper looked more qualified, but God chose you. Even with your past *He intentionally chose you* for the vision.

Queen while you are walking out the vision you may have moments of struggle. You may question the vision or even the purpose in the vision. Know when it's God given nothing anyone says or does can stop it from coming to fruition. Sometimes waiting on the promises takes more faith than believing for the promise.

You must be willing to look crazy to those who know you. Willing to step out and do the work to help your vision come to past, willing to let go of the familiar and step out into the deep. You must believe every word that God speaks to you regarding the vision and be willing to bury yourself deep into His Word.

Stop overthinking how the vision is going to work, that's God's lane. You are trying to be in a lane that was not created for you to move in. God does not need your help. Why do you feel the need to help God? Why do you feel the need to point God in the right direction? The answer is simple yet maybe a little too honest. You simply don't trust God.

The person I was talking about earlier is Noah and the vision was Ark. The Ark is a huge boat that was to survive the flood that God was sending to the earth. God gave Noah the vision, and instructions for the ark when there wasn't a cloud in the sky. When to the natural eye, it made no sense for him to build a boat, let alone a boat the size of which Noah built.

God picked a person who could handle the pressure of the naysayers. Noah had to be useable prior to the vision being complete, while in the process of completion and when it was done. Noah didn't just build the Ark, he lived in the Ark for a little over a year. He didn't leave the Ark until God told him it was time. *Queen* that's the thing about a vision from God *you must wait until God tells you it's time.* People will try and put their time frame on God's vision but often this just creates more of a problem. God knows the perfect time for everything to happen. You just have to put in the work and God will handle the timing.

Psalm 27:14
Here's what I've learned through it all: Don't give up; don't be impatient; be entwined as one with the Lord. Be brave and courageous, and never lose hope. Yes, keep on waiting—for he will never disappoint you!
The Passion Translation (TPT)

Visions Are Not One Size Fit All

Therefore, Noah was the right person for that vision. I don't know if I would have been okay with being in a closed in area for over a year with two of every animal. Can you imagine the smell? I get irritable if I am in my home too long.

It's okay though because I was not created for that vision. That vision was handpicked for Noah. I would not have succeeded in it because it was not for me. The key to completing a vision is making sure the vision you are trying to complete is one that assigned to you by God.

Too many times **Queen**s you are frustrated with a vision God never assigned to you. No, you heard about this vision your friend was doing so you decided you would try this vision as well. *Visions are not one size fits all.* In knowing yourself you must know and understand not every vision is made for you. Trying to insert yourself into a vision that was not created for you will lead you to a place of being burnt out, frustrated, and disappointed with God.

God has to be author of your vision. What God has called you to do might not fit the vision you thought but it is your vision. God may choose to move you in a different direction. Your vision might have been to be married at 25 but God's vision for your life has you still single in your mid 30's.

Stop trying to add to the vision of God and simply embrace it. Noah's God given vision saved not only his life but that of his wife, sons, and their wives. See God's vision for Noah was greater than just Noah. That's how God moves. God's vision for your life will not just impact you but also others attached to you. God's vision for your life is bigger than anything you could imagine.

Psalm 139:17-18
[17] How precious also are Your thoughts to me, O God! How vast is the sum of them! [18] If I could count them, they would outnumber the sand. When I awake, I am still with You.
Amplified Bible (AMP)

Tresniece Perry

*Queen*s stop trying to be anything other than you. You were not created to wear the heels of another *Queen*. Your vision is specially created for you, don't mess it up by adding someone else's anointing, movement, and thoughts to the vision. *Queen* God knew exactly who and what you'd bring when He created the vision for you.

Queen stop boxing God in. God gives you a vision and immediately you want to control who will be a part of the vision, the date and time when the vision will be completed, and how it will be completed. We are so busy planning God visions and promises that we often times forget to trust the journey of the vision. Then when our plan, NOT God's plan, doesn't work we look to blame God when He didn't get the details we added our own. God will move in the opposite direction you think He should move just to prove to you He is God and in control. By boxing God in you limit His movement and flow.

The vision God has for you will not fit your current reality. God will give you a billionaire vision while you are still living in a thousandaire space. *That's just how God works.* He does not take in account your reality when promising you HIS reality.

In the Bible God was not big on giving the details of the vision when He was assigning the vision to its carrier. He simply gave direction and expected people to follow. It was not until people started to follow that God would give additional instructions. He told Noah to build the Arc but only gave basic instructions. He told Moses to free His people but only gave basic instructions. He told Paul to feed his people again only giving basic instructions. All throughout time God has been directing His people by giving visions and promises but still requiring His people to trust the process to completion of the vision.

The requirement often is what gets us **Queen**s in trouble. The ability to *trust with only limited knowledge.* Currently, in this world information can be found with the click of a button but when it comes to God - the Internet cannot help. One must be willing to take Him at His Word, knowing He will not let them fall.

By applying faith to a faith-based vision you grant God permission to act on your behalf. You embrace the plan and movement God has for you. It's time **Queen** to remove your reality and embrace His.

Once you embrace this reality you will understand and accept that God says you are worthy. You are worthy of obtaining every promise and vision God has mapped out for your life. **Queen**, flaws and all you are worthy!

You're Worthy
You're Chosen
You Are Defined by Who God
Says You Are

Worth: having monetary or material value

Self-Esteem: a confidence and satisfaction in oneself

Chosen: one who is the object of choice or of divine favor; an elect person

1 Peter 2:9-12
9-10 But you are the ones chosen by God, chosen for the high calling of priestly work, chosen to be a holy people, God's instruments to do his work and speak out for him, to tell others of the night-and-day difference he made for you—from nothing to something, from rejected to accepted. The Message (MSG)

Girl Fix Your Crown

Before we get into this chapter can you do an honest self-test?

Self-Test 1: Stand in front of mirror without any clothes on. What are the first thoughts of yourself that come to mind? Do these thoughts speak of your beauty from the inside out? Do your thoughts find every "flaw" that has been set by you and the world? Do you know how beautiful you are? So many times, we allow others opinion of us to define our beauty.

_____

_____

_____

_____

Self-Test 2: Take a piece of paper and make two columns (or use the space provided below). Title one column as love and the other column as hate (yes, I know this is a very strong word). In each column list the things you love about yourself and the things you hate about yourself. Which list is longer? Which list was easier to write?

Love	Hate

*Y*our ability to see your self-worth starts with you.

How you paint you, matters. **Queen** no matter how many times someone says you are beautiful unless you believe it for yourself it does not matter. The reason for the self-worth test was for you to be honest about how you see you. Beyond the likes on social media, beyond the "beat face", beyond your relationship status how do you see yourself? What is your self-worth?

These two tests were not an issue for you as you see yourself in the exact flawless state God created; however, for others you have not even made it past the self-test parts. You cannot even image standing in front of mirror at all and looking at yourself. **Queen** we have allowed the media to define our beauty. We base the level of our beauty on how many likes we get on social media. Did you know that beauty is not defined by how "beat" your face is or how well you dress?

1 Samuel 16:7
But God told Samuel, "Looks aren't everything. Don't be impressed with his looks and stature. I've already eliminated him. God judge's persons differently than humans do. Men and women look at the face; God looks into the heart."
The Message (MSG)

David is one of the most well-known biblical figures in the Bible. David was a handsome man by some standards but that didn't matter to his father and brothers. In David's house he was the afterthought, the one nobody really paid any attention. Today, we would call David the "black sheep" of the family. No one considered David in matters of the family or anything.

How difficult it must have been to grow up in a household where not even your father (the person that is supposed to love you and take care of you) doesn't look out for you. To live in a household where you were treated as if you were nothing. David's story like many of you reading this, it is the story of being in the world but nobody really seeing you.

Your birth represents pain and frustration. You grew up in a home where you were treated so bad you often asked God why? Why didn't your mother or father love you, why your skin color is darker that of your siblings, why is my hair nappy instead of straight, why am I so tall or so short?

Queen your inability to love all of you opens the doors for the enemy to come and attack your mind. Let me explain. When you truly love yourself, there are some behaviors you simply will not put up with. In my journey to love myself I often found myself settling because I wanted to be accepted. I settled for incomplete love instead of demanding total love.

The problem with not knowing or accepting your worth is, you put yourself in a place to be treated less than who God called you to be. When I started to walk in my worth some people didn't understand it. Some people accused me of thinking I was all that. Both things were okay because I was finally in a place where I allowed God to show me my worth.

Tresniece Perry

Your beauty is directly tied to your image of yourself. The inability to love all of you instead of pieces of you creates a toxic environment within yourself that leads you down a path of struggle and destructive behavior. Your behaviors reflect your need to be accepted and approved. The issue is you seek these things from people who cannot provide the very thing you seek. Often times we as women turn to the approval of men to prove our worth. We place value in a job or our status in the church to prove our worth.

Created in His Image

Isaiah 64:8

8 Still, God, you are our Father. We're the clay and you're our potter: All of us are what you made us.

The Message (MSG)

You were created in the perfect image of God. Everything from your hair to your shape was hand designed by God. God made no mistakes in your design. His approach to you is similar to the potter. The potter doesn't just slap some clay onto a wheel and spin it around a few times and say it's complete.

No, the potter spends time ensuring His creation is one of kind. Special attention is given to the details to make sure each piece is special. This is the same process God took in making you. You are not some afterthought. Just the opposite, you are God's creation and heartbeat.

Queen you are WORTHY! Stop for a moment and say the following:

- ✓ I am WORTHY of being loved.
- ✓ I am WORTHY of real friendships
- ✓ I am WORTHY of God's favor
- ✓ I AM WORTHY of God's Promises.

No matter how many times you have messed up or how many flaws you have you are still WORTHY.

Proverbs 3:15-18
She is more precious than rubies; And nothing you can wish for compares with her [in value].
Amplified Bible (AMP)

You Are Chosen

Queen God chose you. Guess what? He knows about the abortion and He still chose you. He knows about the failed marriage and He still chose you. He knows about the rape and molestation and He still chose you. See God's choice of you is not based on the surface, nope, God chose you because of what He placed on the inside of you. And no matter what detours your life has taken, none of it has made you unworthy to be chosen and used by God. Your self-worth should reflect your heart's posture not what you look like.

Did you know God thought so much of you that He paid a high ransom for you? God's desire for you to belong to Him was paid with the blood of His Son. God wanted you to be able to come to Him and a have relationship. He wanted you to know how special you are.

Tresniece Perry

Isaiah 43:4

The Holy of Israel, your Savior. I paid a huge price for you: all of Egypt, with rich Cush and Seba thrown in! That's how much you mean to me! That's how much I love you! I'd sell off the whole world to get you back, trade the creation just for you.

The Message (MSG)

There is nothing that you could ever do that would change the way God feels about you. God is totally and completely in love with you. I understand this might be hard to believe because you know your stuff. You know the mistakes you have made and the times you have turned your back on God, yet God still chooses to love you. Your self-worth is NOT determined by how well you live this life. This is the story of a woman in the book of Luke (Luke 7:37-50) who for all the world's reasons was not fit to be in the same room as Jesus, let alone wash His feet.

This woman understands better than anyone why she shouldn't be allowed to be in the presence of God. Yet, when she had the opportunity to show Jesus how much she appreciated Him, she did so by washing His feet with her tears and a really expensive bottle of perfume. The people around Jesus questioned both the woman and Jesus' acceptance of her gesture. The expectation was for God to treat her like everyone else. To only see her for the flaws she carried. Jesus' approach to her was one of acceptance and love. Jesus tells her all of your sins are forgiven and then He grants her peace.

Luke 7:48-50

[48] Then Jesus said to the woman at his feet, "All your sins are forgiven." [49] All the dinner guests said among themselves,

"Who is the one who can even forgive sins?" [50] Then Jesus said to the woman, "Your faith in me has given you life. Now you may leave and walk in the ways of peace."
The Passion Translation (TPT)

Queen this woman understood that she was a mess, but she also understood that Jesus was her way to a better life. *Queen* what your past looks like is only one chapter of your life. Don't' let this one chapter determine your worth. God is not done writing the story of your life. *You are still valuable* to God and God's kingdom. There is still something for you to offer to God. God needs you to be a part of the kingdom. There are other *Queen*s who are waiting on your story. There are other *Queen*s that need to know you can survive the abuse and still make it.

Queen make the decision today to live everyday owning your beauty. Never again will you stand in the shadow of everyone's definition of beauty for you. For the Bible says you are fearfully and wonderfully made! **(Psalms 149:13)** You were created in His image. **(Genesis 1:27)**

Stop Rejecting God

Do you know every time you complain about something on your body you are telling God He sucked at creating you? Every time you say something bad about yourself you reject God. You are telling God that His work is flawed. How can we serve a perfect God yet question the creation that was made in His image?

His creation and choosing of you is powerful. He gave thought to the color of your eyes and the texture of your hair. He gave thought to where you would live and where you would grow up. *He put thought into every fiber of you.* The bible says He knows the number of hairs on your head. *God makes no mistakes and that includes you.* Stop embracing your flaws and looking at them as if they disqualify you. For it's because of your flaws that you are useable to God. You matter to God, all of you, flaws included.

Luke 12:6-7

6–7 "What is the value of your soul to God? Could your worth be defined by an amount of money? God doesn't abandon or forget even the small sparrow he has made. How then could he forget or abandon you? What about the seemingly minor issues of your life? Do they matter to God? Of course, they do! So, you never need to worry, for you are more valuable to God than anything else in this world.
The Passion Translation (TPT)

Perfection

Trying to be perfect or the desire to be perfect is result of an underlying cause. In other words, it's not the root of the problem, it's more like the result of problem. We strive for perfection because we never want to feel the sting of disappointment or the pain of the rejection.

Perfection is our choice because you have made yourself believe "if I do everything right, if I dot every I and cross every T if I am the perfect wife maybe this time my husband won't cheat." Maybe, just maybe if I am perfect than no one will see the scars from years of abuse I suffered. No one will see the shame from the rape or the molestation. No one will know about the drug and alcohol abuse. I have to be perfect in every area. *Queen*, you put the pressure on yourself to be the perfect wife, mother, employee, church member, minister, etc. to measure up. We adopt the mindset if we are perfect then no one will see the cracks in our "perfect life".

As much as the world has benefited from social media you have to keep in mind it's all make believe. On social media everyone has the perfect life. Marriages are happy, kids are great all the time, families are never having money troubles, single people are traveling the world. There is never a bad day on social media. It's the perfect world. The problem is for every marriage that seems to be perfect there is another one that is falling apart. For all of the perfection seen on social media you are still dying on the inside. Your desire to present this perfect life is slowly killing you.

Perfection is false, for not one of us is perfect. There are flaws in each of us and thank God because those flaws are the reasons God sent His Son down here. God knew that we were going to mess up, yet His love for us makes us perfect. God knew we would have a bad day yet, *His love makes us perfect.* The only perfect person to walk this earth was Jesus. He was spotless which is why He was God's **PERFECT CHOICE** to die for our mistakes. It's because of Jesus that in God we are made perfect.

Philippians 3:12
Not that I have already obtained it [this goal of being Christlike] or have already been made perfect, but I actively press on [a]so that I may take hold of that [perfection] for which Christ Jesus took hold of me and made me His own.
Amplified Bible (AMP)

Tresniece Perry

Purpose and Plan

Jeremiah 29:11

I know what I'm doing. I have it all planned out—plans to take care of you, not abandon you, plans to give you the future you hope for.

The Message (MSG)

The devil understood long before I did what **PURPOSE AND PLAN** God had for my life. The devil knew what was growing on the inside of me since my mother's womb was a **PURPOSE** and **PLAN.** While the devil didn't know the exact plan of what God had for me, he understood this plan would involve me being able to receive unconditional love and also able to give it.

Queen the same is for you. There is a plan which God has mapped out just for you. It's a **PURPOSE** that only you can fulfill, no one else. It was handcrafted, developed, and shaped with you in mind. That's why the distractions have been so intense and certain people could not be a part of your forever.

Know and embrace that your **PURPOSE** didn't stop because you took a detour or two in your life. It's just the opposite, *God worked your detour into your PURPOSE.* Have you ever been driving in the car and you start using some form of GPS? The GPS system tells you to make a right but instead you make a left? The system does not shut off because you made the wrong turn. No, the system simply finds a way for you to get you back on track. It may require you to make a U-turn or turn down a different street. If may even adjust the original route for the destination by saying "rerouting" to still get you to the appointed place.

Girl Fix Your Crown

God is the same way and His intent is for you to reach your appointed place. God wants you to get the promise. He wants your life to reflect His love for you and if that means rerouting you a few times He will. If that means adding a few more miles to your journey He will. God is intent on what He put on the inside of you to be birthed.

This **PURPOSE AND PLAN** is why the job didn't work out. There was a time when I would get mad if a job I applied for didn't hire me, but not anymore. Now I just agree with God it must not have been part of my **PURPOSE.** When the guy that I just knew was going to my husband didn't notice my worth I stopped getting mad because I now realize they were not attached to my **PURPOSE.**

Stop trying to make the job, that man, the ministry, the relationship part of your **PURPOSE.** For if God did not intend for it to be, no matter how many scriptures you quote, no matter how many times you shout and fall out, if God said no then it's a no. Either live with it or deal with the consequences later.

Jeremiah 29:10-11
10-11 This is GOD's Word on the subject: "As soon as Babylon's seventy years are up and not a day before, I'll show up and take care of you as I promised and bring you back home. I know what I'm doing. I have it all planned out—plans to take care of you, not abandon you, plans to give you the future you hope for.
The Message (MSG)

Tresniece Perry

King: Date Like A

Queen

Dating: to make a usually romantic social arrangement to meet with; to have a date with

Courting: be involved with romantically, typically with the intention of marrying

Marriage: a: the state of being united as spouses in a consensual and contractual relationship recognized by law
b: the mutual relation of married persons; wedlock
c: the institution whereby individuals are joined in a marriage

Proverbs 18:22
Find a good spouse, you find a good life—and even more: the favor of God!
The Message (MSG)

*D*uring a recent conversation I was asked, have I ever been courted before. Confused I asked is that any different than dating? I have heard of the term of courting before, but I was not totally familiar with the term but not sure if I had ever experienced it.

Her response was dating is more of a getting to know you, but it includes the man getting to know other people as well, whereas courting is more one on one and exclusive. With that knowledge I told her no I have never been courted before. To say she was shocked was an understatement and she even went as far to state "that's sad."

Just like many girls I often spent time dreaming about my wedding day. Where would it happen, how would my dress look. I often thought what would the groom look like? Would he attend my church home? What would the colors be? How many people would I invite, and the thoughts and questions would go on and on. I never really gave any thought to the marriage but just that one day. Yet here I am a 38-year-old, never been married and made to acknowledge never being courted. Leaving her office, I could not shake the question or the uneasiness it left me with.

Frustrated because I think, does she think that I wanted to be single at 38? I have been in more weddings than I care to admit to. Even in my career as a Makeup Artist I now help give brides the most important look they will have on their wedding day. Yet, I am no closer to being married or courted. It's seemed this desire was one God kept overlooking.

Tresniece Perry

I've dated my share of gentleman but never made it to the courting stage. Why is that? One of the major answers is simple but POWERFUL and true. *I simply took God out of it.* In both my heart and mind, I told God He was not qualified to handle this part of my life. Now before you shake your head at me and ask how I could say that, read my story.

In 2005, I was told I was being prepared for marriage. I remember the exact moment when I was given this awesome news. Finally, my secret prayer was being answered. My brain started to draw the picture of who I thought the perfect guy would be; however, just as I was imagining him I was told "No, it's not him". Huh was my response because I know I didn't say anything, yet her response was the same "no, it's not him."

Well if he was not God's choice I decided to cut off all communications with him and any other guy. I was on a mission to the altar. I begin to do everything in my power to make sure I was in top position for the blessing God had said he was giving me. I attended every church service, and I became overly active in the church. I became a super saint.

I was so busy trying to make sure I was "perfect" for God's promise that I lost sight of the fact God gave me the promise. In 2007, in the month of July the first Saturday of that month was 7-7-07. That was it. The perfect day for God's promise to come to past.

Wrong - God never promised me I would be married on that Saturday. Matter fact God never even gave me a date. All He told me was that I was being prepared for marriage, the rest of it I added on to it. As you can image when the day came and went I was filled with such disappointment, I was hurt but even beyond that I was angry with God. It was the first time I felt like God played me. I felt like He dangled a carrot (my dream of marriage) got me all excited and then yanked it from my reach.

As a result, (of what I thought was God's failure) I said to God you can't handle this part of my life. I trusted you and you let me down. I said God you will never hurt me like this again. Now, while I didn't say this out of my mouth (let's be real He is still God) in my heart, mind, and actions I did. I stopped asking God about the men I would meet. I stopped inquiring with God if these men were meant to be in my life and in what role.

Queen, my truth in that moment was: I don't trust God in matters of my heart. I didn't trust God to move in His timing, get all the bullet points on my check list, I didn't trust that God really knew best when it came to me and I didn't trust God with my important stuff. Sure, I trusted Him with other areas of my life, but this area was off limits.

Trusting God to handle finding my husband was a no go. Telling God, I trust Him with my words and on paper is a lot different than trusting Him with my actions and dreams. It was easier to just remove God from this area of my life. With every wedding I attended or bridal shower I was invited too I felt justified in my position to block God out. I felt like it was okay, and God had no say so in my dating world. I could find my Mr. Right. I knew me, I know what I like and don't like. I know my wants better than anyone else.

Tresniece Perry

This experience was like the experience Sarah faced when she went to help God with His promise. In the book of Genesis 15 God made a promise to Abraham (Abram at the time) that He (God) would give him a child from his own seed. In Chapter 16 Sarah (Sarai) decided to help God with His plan by having her husband sleep with her handmaid a woman named Hagar to give Abraham the child God had promised.

Sarah added to what God said and just like in my case - things did not go as planned. For Sarah became upset when Hagar got pregnant. She treated her so bad that Hagar had to leave Sarah.

God does not need our help when it comes to any promise that He makes us. He doesn't require us to join any sites or go on multiple dates in order to find the right one. God is intentional in all that He does even when it comes to us getting married.

Our "helping" of God and His promises delay the promises, and also serves to create more obstacles for God to work around. As stated in this chapter and others you have to **TRUST GOD and HIS TIMING!**

2 Peter 3:8-9

Nevertheless, do not let this one fact escape your notice, beloved, that with the Lord one day is like a thousand years, and a thousand years is like one day. 9 The Lord does not delay [as though He were unable to act] and is not slow about His promise, as some count slowness, but is [extraordinarily] patient toward you, not wishing for any to perish but for all to come to repentance.

Amplified Bible (AMP)

With my new goal of removing God and finding my Mr. Right…where did this leave me? That's an easy answer: more dates but no courting. I was left with a broken heart more times than I care to talk about, a self-esteem that took a beating, and finally I was left asking God why didn't it work out this time over and over?

My new way of living created more questions than answers and found me lowering my standards and just being happy when the guy did the bare minimum. By removing God from this part of my life, what I was really doing was opening myself up to be beat up and played with by the devil over and over again. Please know when you take God out of an area of your life you leave the space free for the devil to play.

Looking back to that day in 2005, I immediately started to add to God's promise. Even to the point when God said it was not the person I wanted it to be I remember praying God would change His mind. I was so intent on getting what God said at any cost I never stopped to think about God. I just wanted to be married that is all that mattered. The quality of the man didn't matter.

Queens we mess up when we try to help God with His promise. When we try to "coach" God in moving and acting how we want him to act. *God does not need our help!* God's intent is just not in us getting what we want but it's more based on our needs changing and impacting the Kingdom of God (yes, even in marriage). It stopped mattering to me what God wanted because all I could see was what I wanted.

God knew even at the expense of my feelings and emotions His desire for me to be completely and totally whole on the inside mattered more than my five-year tantrum I was having, even if lasted for almost 10 years. God never let me get too far left and quickly ended any situation that seemed to push me further from Him. God being the gentleman He is never forced my hand. Every time I felt as if my heart was being ripped in two He extended me **GRACE** and **MERCY** by loving on me a little hard that day. Even when I promised I was ready to let him go or I was ready to stop "helping" I would soon get tired of waiting and go back to the vomit of failed relationships.

By this time the disappointment and hurt had shifted to bitterness and anger. So, I no longer spoke on this desire to anyone. Thank you but the advice of "as soon as you stop looking he will find you" was overkill. Thank you but the books people kept giving me were now collecting dust on my bookshelf - some I never even opened. No placing it on the vision boards. No more praying for my husband (that I said may or may not come). The bitterness and anger at God over the situation was slowly turning into a poison I drank daily.

When I would be in a situation or a conversation about marriage, my response would be "if I get married or if have a wedding". Maybe it was my way of moving past the hurt and the feelings I had attached to marriage or my desire to get married. After one too many heartbreaks I told God that's it. I was officially giving this part of my life back over to Him, but I was honest to say God I need your help.

A few months before I really committed to writing this book I found myself having a random conversation (at least I thought it was random) with one of my mentors. She proceeds to ask me a question.

It was a question I had been asked often and one I had a ready answer for.

"Why did I want to be married so desperately?" My response was "I have always wanted to be married." This was my standard response, but she came back with a "why." Again, I stated, "I have always wanted to be married for as far back as I can remember". Her reply was "Why does that seem to be so important to you?" I sat and for the first time I had no answer. Deep down I had no answer as to why being married was so important to me. It just always was. Her next comment went straight to my heart and spirit. In this moment, I knew it was not her talking but God talking through her. She said, "you equate marriage with being worthy." I was stuck, and I had no reply because for the first time ever I knew why marriage was so important to me.

Yes, the thought of marriage and worth went hand and hand for me. It was something about a man thinking enough of me to say I was worthy of his love, his time, and his last name. There was something to him finding me more special than all the other women in the world. This is why I wanted marriage so bad because I wanted to feel worthy of being loved.

Marriage validated my worth. The issue with this flawed thinking is it made me incompatible for the kind of man God wanted to bring into my life. Brokenness will only attract brokenness. The problem was not them (the guys I was dating or attracting) it was me. As long as my flawed thinking had room to grow and I fed it, marriage would be off the table.

Tresniece Perry

Now this explained why I never COURTED and I only DATED. **Queen**, I first needed to be honest about the part that I played in this. When God told me, He was preparing me for marriage I saw wedding. I thought of the wedding day not the marriage. I thought about colors and the wedding dress but gave little in terms of the quality of the man. God does nothing half way. He intent was to ensure that I not only had an awesome wedding day but that I had an even better marriage. For that to happen God had to do a work on the inside of me.

Had I gotten married when I thought I was ready - here is what I know for sure: I would either be miserable, or I would be divorced right now. Basing my worth on my marriage would have meant that I would have put expectations on my husband that he would not have been able to fulfill. It would have been like me placing CEO expectations on the janitor.

He would have failed every time. He was not created for that role, to be my reason for my worth. Due to this I would have been setting both myself and our marriage up to fail. Only God can give me my worth and only I have the power to accept it. This task is not made for my husband. His love should affirm what I already know to be true about myself, I should not be seeking him for it. The same for you **Queen**!

God needed me to understand that my worth was set by Him and not by the man I am dating or married too. God needed me to understand that I am worthy of love not just because some man asked me to marry him but because God says I am worthy. **Queen**, this is the same for you. You are not less than because you are not married. Your worth is not tied to a ring on your left hand.

Get to the place where you are okay waiting for God to send you the King He created just for you. Stop apologizing for requiring people to treat you as the *Queen* you are. No more making excuses or settling for being a runner up. Understand you set the standard on how you want to be treated.

Proverbs 3:15 says, "She is more precious than rubies; And nothing you can wish for compares with her [in value]. Amplified Bible (AMP)

Place your name where the word "she" is. Know for yourself *Queen* you are more precious than rubies. Nothing compares to your value.

Now with this new found understanding of your worth when it comes to COURTING the question remains, what it COURTING? An even better question is, what does it look like? Let's compare them:

DATING	COURTING
Open to multiple people	Specific to a person
No commitment	Goal directed-marriage
Sex is ok	No go on sex
Dates are often just the two of you	Dating is often in groups: this can be up to the couple
You can see other people	Seeking God's opinion
Doesn't really include God	Male Leads: Allowing the guy to chase
No plan	Committed Relationship

If it's your desire is to be married, then you should desire courting not just dating. Courting is going to require more patience and trust in God. I have often heard; how will you ever find a husband if you don't get out there? I bought into this theory and so I got out there. Even joined a dating site or two (more like all of them) I didn't get a husband, but I did go on a few dates. Dating can be fun but where is it leading?

King Ready

The Radiant Bride The Passion Translation (Proverbs 31: 10-31)

[10] **Who could ever find a wife like this one—**
she is a woman of strength and mighty valor!
She's full of wealth and wisdom.
The price paid for her was greater than many jewels.
[11] **Her husband has entrusted his heart to her,**
for she brings him the rich spoils of victory.
[12] **All throughout her life she brings him what is good and not evil.**
[13] **She searches out continually to possess**
that which is pure and righteous.
She delights in the work of her hands.
[14] **She gives out revelation-truth to feed others.**
She is like a trading ship bringing divine supplies
from the merchant.
[15] **Even in the night season she arises and sets food on the table**
for hungry ones in her house and for others.
[16] **She sets her heart upon a nation and takes it as her own,**
carrying it within her.

She labors there to plant the living vines.

[17] She wraps herself in strength, might, and power in all her works.

[18] She tastes and experiences a better substance,
   and her shining light will not be extinguished,
   no matter how dark the night.

[19] She stretches out her hands to help the needy
   and she lays hold of the wheels of government.

[20] She is known by her extravagant generosity to the poor,
   for she always reaches out her hands to those in need.

[21] She is not afraid of tribulation,
   for all her household is covered in the dual garments
   of righteousness and grace.

[22] Her clothing is beautifully knit together—
   a purple gown of exquisite linen.

[23] Her husband is famous and admired by all,
   sitting as the venerable judge of his people.

[24] Even her works of righteousness
   she does for the benefit of her enemies.

[25] Bold power and glorious majesty are wrapped around her
   as she laughs with joy over the latter days.

[26] Her teachings are filled with wisdom and kindness
   as loving instruction pours from her lips.

[27] She watches over the ways of her household
   and meets every need they have.

[28] Her sons and daughters arise in one accord to extol her virtues,
   and her husband arises to speak of her in glowing terms.

[29] "There are many valiant and noble ones,
   but you have ascended above them all!"

[30] Charm can be misleading,

and beauty is vain and so quickly fades,

but this virtuous woman lives in the wonder, awe,

and fear of the Lord.

She will be praised throughout eternity.

[31] So go ahead and give her the credit that is due,

for she has become a radiant woman,

and all her loving works of righteousness deserve to be admired

at the gateways of every city!

Queen are you praying for something you are not ready for? Are you praying for a King but presenting yourself to be a peasant? The portion of scripture listed above talks about a woman a King meets who has the criteria of a godly wife. Her family is taken care of. She is handling the business side of things for the family. Her husband feels safe with her. He trusts her to conduct herself as the *Queen* she is at all times. The scripture goes on to ask the question. Who can find her? Asking the question does she exist and the answer to the question is yes, she does. She is you and you are her. You are the woman that some man somewhere is praying for and covering in his prayers. You are the woman who can take care of home and the business.

Does this require work-YES! Does this mean there will be sometimes when you must "court" yourself-YES. Take yourself to a nice restaurant. Go see your favorite new movie! Keep your nails and feet done (even if you do it at home). Keep your hair done! Work on your credit.

Make sure you have let go of past hurts and rejections. Don't bring that baggage into your courtship with your King. *Queen* empty out your emotional bags. Get rid of any soul ties. Make sure there is room in your heart for your King. The outward stuff you can take care of but in order to be what this scripture is talking about you MUST ALLOW GOD to do His complete and total work on the inside. This is a process, but it is one that is worth it!

God is Creating Your King

Genesis 2:18
18 Now the Lord God said, "It is not good (beneficial) for the man to be alone; I will make him a helper [one who balances him—a counterpart who is] [a]suitable and complementary for him."
Amplified Bible (AMP)

Just as God is requiring you to work on yourself, know God is working on creating the perfect King for you. God is taking special attention to making sure your King can handle all parts of you. God wants to ensure your King will not be intimidated with the **PURPOSE** and **PLAN** He created on the inside of you.

This is why you cannot just date anyone. Your destiny will not allow you to be matched to someone because he is cute. No, God is requiring more for your King because your impact on Kingdom with your marriage is that important. Stop rushing the process or trying make the janitor your CEO. He is not eligible to be your King so stop trying to make it so.

Soul Ties

Matthew 19:5 says, "For this cause shall a man leave father and mother and shall cleave to his wife: and they twain shall be one flesh."

Have you ever dated someone and even when it was over you couldn't seem to get over them? No matter how hard you tried your mind and heart always went back to them? The way they ate or how they smelled. If a certain song came on the radio it made you think of them. You found yourself comparing anyone you met to them.

For some there is a connection to them that you cannot explain (even if the relationship or situationship ended badly). There is just something there. You have prayed that God would remove it, but it seems to still be there. You have dated other people, but it still seems to be there. The reason is a soul tie was created. A soul tie can be created both in relationships of the opposite sex or even in simple friendships. For this part of the book we will only look at the relationship side of it.

There is a reason why God created sex for marriage. It's not because He wanted to deprive us of pleasure (nope he created the desire and pleasure that we have on the inside) it's because God understood that every time you and a person give yourself intimately to each other you leave a part of yourself and you take a piece of them.

A soul tie is the knitting of two souls together. It's more than just you having a good 15 or 20 minutes of pleasure, its attaching your emotions, thoughts, and soul together to someone. A soul tie can be both beneficial and harmful but not at the same time. When a soul tie is created in a God induced situation (inside of a Godly marriage) then the soul tie draws the man and woman together. Just the opposite a soul tie in a harmful situation can keep two people together who should not be together.

How are soul ties created?

1. **Sex:** any sexual relationship creates a soul tie in or out of marriage

2. **Close Friendships:** spending a lot of time with someone to the point where you start to think and act alike

3. **Vows:** Things like I swear I will never love anyone the way I loved you. Saying stuff like I promise to only…. with you, creates a soul tie

Breaking Soul Ties:

Soul ties can be broken no matter how they were created. The first step is deciding if you really want the soul tie to be broken. Making the choice to no longer desire anything from that person.

1. Renounce any sin that caused the soul tie (sex outside of marriage tends to be the most common) If no sin exists that is okay as well.

2. Getting rid of anything that was given. Love letter, gifts, if you wore a certain bra set or lingerie set for them. Anything that holds memories you need to get rid of. I know this step seems drastic especially if you received some nice stuff but look at it this way;

why would you want to hold onto anything that caused you pain and suffering?

3. Forgive the person: We spoke on this **Queen** in another chapter. Forgiveness is never just for them it's really for you. Let go of the pain and hurt that is attached to them. Let go of the memories.

4. Renounce the soul tie. Do this verbally, and in Jesus' name. Example: "In Jesus' name, I now renounce any ungodly soul ties formed between myself and _____ as a result of _____ (fornication, etc.)."

5. Break the soul tie in Jesus' name! Do this verbally using your authority in Jesus. Example: "I now break and sever any ungodly soul ties formed between myself and _____ as a result of _____ (fornication, etc.) in Jesus' name."

The Queen's Court:

Religion, Relationships &

Friendships

Relationship: (1) the state of being related or interrelated
(2) the relation connecting or binding participants in a relationship:
such as a: kinship b: a specific instance or type of kinship
(3) a: a state of affairs existing between those having relations or
dealings b: a romantic or passionate attachment

Religion: (1) the service and worship of God or the supernatural
(2) commitment or devotion to religious faith or observance; a
personal set or institutionalized system of religious attitudes, beliefs,
and practices (3) a belief in the being and perfections of God, in the
revelation of his will to man, in man's obligation to obey his
commands, in a state of reward and punishment, and in man's
accountability to God; and also, true godliness

Tresniece Perry

98

(4) a cause, principle, or system of beliefs held to with ardor and faith

John 15:12-15
"This is My commandment, that you love and unselfishly seek the best for one another, just as I have loved you. [13] No one has greater love [nor stronger commitment] than to lay down his own life for his friends. [14] You are my friends if you keep on doing what I command you. [15] I do not call you servants any longer, for the servant does not know what his master is doing; but I have called you [My] friends, because I have revealed to you everything that I have heard from My Father.
Amplified Bible (AMP)

*A*s we go through life we build many relationships and

connections over time.

Some connections were meant to last a lifetime, others were more seasonal. There are connections that were made where you were meant to learn and have things planted or connections you were there to water what someone else already planted. Throughout each connection, a type of relationship was created.

In Luke 5:17-26 where Jesus is teaching and the house where he is teaching is so packed there is no room to get to Jesus. There is a man who is a paraplegic who was healed by God not based on his faith and actions but on the actions and faith of those he was connected to. In the Bible it tells us that the "power of the Lord was present to heal". This man had friends who were determined to get him before Jesus.

When they approached the house and saw there was no way to carry him through a door they came up with a plan of their own. They cut a hole in the roof and lowered the shaking man in front of Jesus. His friends were not concerned with the opinions of others. They did not concern themselves with the whispers from the people who had gathered. No, due to the relationship they had with this man none of the other stuff mattered; all that mattered was their friend being healed.

My point??? **Queen** *your relationships matter.* The people you create connections with matter. They matter not just to present situations, but they matter to your future as well. Ask yourself the question: does the current connections I have add or take away from my PURPOSE? We must be very careful about the connections we make throughout our journey. We must understand that not all connections are meant to be lifelong connections some are seasonal. Many problems come in when we confuse seasonal relationships with lifelong relationships. When you try to make seasonal relationships lifelong relationships you set yourself up to be let down and disappointed.

Out of all my relationships both present and former the greatest one I have is with Jesus Christ. For through this connection He has granted access to God. It's through my relationship with Jesus that I can have a relationship with God.

John 14:6

Tresniece Perry

Jesus said to him, "[a]I am the [only] Way [to God] and the [real] Truth and the [real] Life; no one comes to the Father but through Me.
Amplified Bible (AMP)

Due to this relationship there is someone who praying on your behalf. Through this relationship I became royalty. I became the daughter of a King. This relationship grants me the access to God through the Holy Spirit. Through this connection my life was forever changed. This relationship gives me peace when I need it and grants love at your weakest point.

God wants more for His children (yes *Queen* you are counted as God's child). He didn't want robots who tried to listen to every command, no *He wanted RELATIONSHIP!* A relationship is different from religion in the fact it includes friendship. That's right *Queen God wants a friendship with you. Queen* is it possible to have a relationship with someone if you don't trust them? No relationship works without trust.

At the age of 12 I got saved and filled with the Holy Ghost. In that moment it was truly (and still is) the best decision I have ever made but if I was honest I would say my idea of salvation and what salvation is were two different things. I thought salvation was a long list (a really long list) of do and don'ts. I thought it was about living this perfect life where I strived to make God happy no matter the cost. I saw it as God standing in heaven waiting for me to mess up so He could zap me.

As a result, I rebelled. I thought it was impossible to please God so why try. Some of my most troubling years happened before I turned 16. I smoked weed and drank. I had the worst mouth ever. All the time making good grades in school, still being respectful to most adults. I snuck boys in the house when my mom was not home.

I lied about the dumbest stuff. I pretended to be a "sex expert" when in reality I was still a virgin who just happened to watch a lot of porn. I did all the "right" stuff so that I could get away with doing my bad stuff. I was trying to fit in. The crazy part was the more I tried to fit in the more it seemed I didn't.

Around the age of 16 I started to change some of my behaviors and wanted to really try God out. So, I went from one extreme to another. I become super saint. I wanted all my friends to go to church. I would "preach" about God at school to anyone that would listen. My style of dress changed, the music I that listened to changed. I no longer wanted to be part of the gossip. I started trying to convert all my friends to get saved. Even with me dotting all my I's and crossing all of my T's something was still missing. Two very different extremes with one common ground, neither one of them spoke about relationship with God.

Romans 3:23-24
Since all have sinned and continually fall short of the glory of God, [24] and are being justified [declared free of the guilt of sin, made acceptable to God, and granted eternal life] as a gift by His [precious, undeserved] grace, through the redemption [the payment for our sin] which is [provided] in Christ Jesus.
Amplified Bible (AMP)

Queen we all have fallen short. At one time or another we all have gossiped about someone, failed to show God's love to the least deserving, and told a lie or two. We have done something that falls under the category of sin and according to the old law (before Christ) we all were not worthy of God's love. This is the reason God sent Jesus to earth. God wanted us to have a gift.

John 3:16

For God so [greatly] loved and dearly prized the world, that He [even] gave His [One and] [a]only begotten Son, so that whoever believes and trusts in Him [as Savior] shall not perish but have eternal life.
Amplified Bible (AMP)

Trust and Relationship

Trust is so important that it comes a few times throughout this book.
Queen in your heart of hearts answer this question:

I trust God because:

_____.

I don't trust God because:

_____.

Now looking at what which one you answered what is the reasoning behind your selection. Did God let you down *Queen*? Did He not answer a prayer that you submitted? Did He make you wait too long for something? The bottom line is that no matter the reason for why, *without trust there can be no relationship with God. Trusting God means being vulnerable to God* and knowing that He will not let you down.

Girl Fix Your Crown

See past experiences have taught me to only let people in so far and this included God. In many cases I was simply giving God the side eye on certain things because I didn't know if He could be trusted. I was still carrying around the scars of broken promises, the residue of rejection, and the entitlement of being the victim. I felt justified in treating my relationship with God as something I could manipulate and control.

Queen how could I have a relationship with God when I was trying to control it. I mean really, how does one control the person that created the heavens and earth? How do I control the person who knows my thoughts even before I do? How do I stand and tell God I love Him but I don't trust him? No relationship can grow, be maintained, and thrive if trust is not in it. *In order to fully trust God, I must be willing to surrender to God everything.*

Surrender and Relationship

Surrender can be both a noun and a verb. It can be defined in the form of a verb as one who must abandon rights to something: or to simply give up. In defining it as a noun one must be willing to give up control. *Queen surrendering is not a form of weakness.* It's just the opposite; it's the biggest form of strength there is. There is nothing stronger than admitting you have come to the end of your rope. The reason is God thrives in these times. The moment when let go God says, "yes finally I can do the work within her." Now she can totally be free. Now she can really start to live this life that I desired for her. Now she is ready to embrace the life that I have for her. Now she is READY to be the *Queen* that I have called her to be.

Tresniece Perry

How many times has God told you to surrender and even though you mouth said yes, your heart said no. *For some of you reading this you have "served" God for a long time but you have yet to "SURRENDER" to God.* Part of being a **Queen** is understanding who created you and that He really wants nothing but the best for you.

Taking this journey with God I now understand why surrendering to His will is so important. I remember as a child I couldn't wait to become an adult because then I would be grown and there would be no one to tell me what to do. I would be able to live my life the way I wanted and not have to answer to anyone. I had it all planned out. I would stay out as long as I wanted (now I am in the bed by 8:30 on most nights). I would watch whatever I wanted on tv (still don't do this). Yes, I going to be my own woman. That was the plan, but God had other plans.

Funny thing is living for God I have reached some different conclusions. I now understand for me to really live *I must be willing to surrender my life* and all its parts to the plans God has for me. I can keep kicking against the grain but in the end all it does is make my life harder. I have stood in church on so many Sunday's and sang songs about surrendering to God, but actions proved I really didn't mean it. *The art of surrender is trust.* There cannot be one without the other.

When you refuse to surrender to God it has a direct impact on your relationship with God. By refusing to surrender you open yourself up to encounter things God never intended for you to have to face. This action results in delays in you getting the promises of God coming to fruition in your life.

Girl Fix Your Crown

In the Bible there is a story about a group of people who God gave the promise of a land flowing with milk and honey but because of their stubbornness only two out of millions made it into the promised land (this the story of the Children of Israel). How is it possible that God could make such a big promise and then only allow two people in to see it? It's simple, by refusing to surrender to God, His ways, and embrace them - the ones who didn't make it forfeited their promises.

God handpicked these people to get this promise. He sent a special massager (Moses) to deliver them from under the hand of Pharaoh, yet due their posture of being stubborn they missed the very thing they were delivered for. **Queen** how crazy is it for you to have gone through all that you have been through to not get what God has instore for you. That is the risk you take when you refuse to surrender to God.

Queen a surrendered heart says: God I surrender to your will because it's the place where I learn You and Your ways. It's the place where you teach me how to love from the heart instead through my actions only. It's the place where you teach me my value! It's the place where your love changes me from the inside out. Surrendering is me saying God you know the final say. God, I trust you with my life since you have already seen the end result. God this life is meant for Your glory so have Your way with it. God, I surrender all to you!!!!!!

Today I ask you are you ready to surrender this life to God? Are you ready to embrace the movement of God even when it doesn't make sense? Surrender and trust are alike in the sense that you cannot have one without the other. **Queen** there is no way that you surrender to someone that you don't trust. Trust in God will cause you to be willing to surrender to God. Thus, opening the door for a solid relationship with God. **Queen** it is all connected. Your relationship with God is only as strong as your level of trust and surrender to God and His will.

A Gift Fit for A Queen

Queen I wanted to take a moment to offer you the greatest gift I have ever received. This gift is life changing. This gift ensures that every day (no matter what happens that day) there is someone praying for you. This gift brings you into a family and accepts your flaws and all. This gift opens the communication between you and your heavenly Father. I want to offer you the gift of Salvation.

This gift is forever and once it is accepted - can never be taken away from you. The key to this gift though is that you must first accept it. God is requesting permission to enter into your heart and reside there for all eternity. This gift has nothing to do with your past but has the power to change and enhance your present and future.

If you are ready to accept this gift, then read this out loud:

I confess that Jesus is Lord.
I believe that He died but rose with all power.
I now accept Jesus as my Lord and Savior forever more.
Amen

Tresniece Perry

Your Salvation Scripture:

Romans 10:9-10

If you declare with your mouth, "Jesus is Lord," and believe in your heart that God raised him from the dead, you will be saved. [10] For it is with your heart that you believe and are justified, and it is with your mouth that you profess your faith and are saved.

New International Version (NIV)

That's it *Queen* you are now part of God's family. Because your heavenly Father is King of Kings that means that you are now royalty. This has been God's plan all along to welcome you into His family.

Ephesians 1:3-6

How blessed is God! And what a blessing he is! He's the Father of our Master, Jesus Christ, and takes us to the high places of blessing in him. Long before he laid down earth's foundations, he had us in mind, had settled on us as the focus of his love, to be made whole and holy by his love. Long, long ago he decided to adopt us into his family through Jesus Christ. (What pleasure he took in planning this!) He wanted us to enter into the celebration of his lavish gift-giving by the hand of his beloved Son.

The Message (MSG)

Remember on this new journey God wants relationship over religion. By accepting this gift, it starts you on the path to a relationship and a friendship with God. Now God will have the opportunity to speak directly to you and provide guidance in your life. **Queen**, this walk is about you and Him. Allow Him the chance to show you how special you are!

Queen Your Crown Is Now

Fixed

Own It

Embrace It

Walk in It

Live It

Thank You

First, I must thank God for entrusting me with this gift.

God your faith in me simply amazes me! This book is truly a gift from you. It started with a title you gave me in a dream. When I moved a little slower than you might have liked you gave me a full color vision of the cover quickly followed by the chapter titles. Once I was fully on board with your vision to writing this book 30 days was all it took. God this is truly all for your Glory! My prayer and belief is that every woman who picks this book up, life will be forever changed. This book God is your love letter to your daughters as you encourage, reaffirm, and empower them to be the **Queen** you created, called, and equipped them to be. Thank you for first doing the work on the inside of me.

Parents:

Mommy and Daddy thank you for being two of my biggest supports. Mommy thank you for instilling in me the power of PRAYER and for introducing me to a relationship with God for without them I would not be here. Thank you for every sacrifice you made so me and my siblings had the best. I often joke mommy, the reason you had knee surgery is because I keep you on your knees praying. I tell you this often - I am the woman I am today because of your love for me.

*D*addy thank you for loving me and supporting all the dreams

I call you about. You made a daddy's girl and even now I know there is nothing you will not do for me (even if that means ordering me pizza from NY). For every mountain you have climbed and every valley you have walked through to be a part of both Betty's, Destini's, and my life THANK YOU! Your journey has not been easy, but I am so glad God honored the prayer of a little girl.

Family:

*T*hank to my all my aunts, uncles and cousins for being family.

No matter how far we live from each other I love you all very much.

Grandma Betty thank you for all the summers in Queens on 131st Street. I spent so much time there I have friends now who swear I am from there and tell me to stop saying I am from DC (even though I really am).

Uncle Sha thanks for being you. There are no words to describe your impact on both Betty and my life. From the regular weekends (more like every weekend) at your house to the family trips we attended you always keep Betty and I with you and made sure we were okay. While you didn't get any daughters of your own God gave you two bonus daughters in both Betty and I. Thanks Sha.

Bro aka Kwane thank you for being my OLDER brother and getting some of my spankings growing up (smile). I know it was hard for you to adjust to being mommies second favorite (don't worry we won't tell Betty) but you handled it well...lol. Love you much!

To my oldest friend and my best secret keeper, thank you for taking this journey with me, Ms. Perry…

Sister Circle:

To my girls Betty (Sissy), Shawnta, (My BFF), Lorice (Parker), Anna (Boss Lady), Sherri (Sherri Berry), Jasmine, Rev. Denise and Rev. Caryn (My Knitted Sisters), Women of Purpose Sunday School Teachers/Sisters (Rev. Katrina, Rev. Vanessa, Rev. Denise, and Rev. Letrice) thank you for being the anchor I needed to birth this project. Your countless support and encouragement means the world to me. You ladies believed in the gift inside of me long before I did and kept pushing me when I wanted to give up. Thank you for your prayers! Rev. Letrice maybe we both will make it to Oprah!

Pastors:

*G*od blessed me many years ago when He gave me Pastor D and Pastor S, my bonus parents. Pastor D thank you for being an example of a cool Pastor. I know I can come to you about anything and when you are finished laughing you will give me an honest dad response. Thank you for your prayers over me and for me. Pastor D thank you for delivering the AWESOME Word of God Sunday after Sunday no matter what you are going through. Thank you for showing me how my husband should love me (minus the whole drinking of the bath water…church joke).

*P*astor S where do I start. I remember the first day I saw you and from the moment I knew you were different and special. Your ability to always see me no matter how much I tried to hide amazes me. You love the W.O.R.D. women with a grace that is unmatched. Thank you, Pastor S, for always being you:

Classy, Anointed, Powerful,

Stunning and Fabulous.

C.P.B.B.C. Family:

Family is the best way to describe you. I have literally grown up with this family. You have seen me go from a child delinquent into the woman I am today. When I stumbled during this journey you found a way to love me anyway. I have way too many aunts and uncles to try and list, so I will say THANK YOU! Every word, every prayer, every stern lecture has lead me to this place. For all the Youth Leaders I gave a run for your money back in the day I am living proof your work was not in vain. Thank you for seeing a young girl who was broken but you loved her anyway.

To All My Fellow Queens:

Thank you for purchasing my first book. Know this book is part of God's plan for your life. I pray this book changes your life as it did mine when I was writing it. As you continue on the journey of becoming who God created you to be remember this. always:

Acknowledge, Embrace and Strut Like a Queen®

References

Scripture quotations marked TPT are from The Passion Translation®. Copyright © 2017, 2018 by Passion & Fire Ministries, Inc. Used by permission. All rights reserved. ThePassionTranslation.com.

All Scripture quotations are from The Passion Translation®. Copyright © 2017, 2018 by Passion & Fire Ministries, Inc. Used by permission. All rights reserved. ThePassionTranslation.com.

"Scripture quotations taken from the Amplified® Bible (AMP), Copyright © 2015 by The Lockman Foundation Used by permission. www.Lockman.org"

"Scripture taken from The Message. Copyright © 1993, 1994, 1995, 1996, 2000, 2001, 2002. Used by permission of NavPress Publishing Group."

All definitions taken from 2011. In Merriam-Webster.com. Retrieved May 2018, from https://www.merriam-webster.com/dictionary/

About the Author

Rev. Tresniece Nicole Perry is a speaker, author, and entrepreneur, Makeup Artist and President and CEO of Divine Faces. Her skills have taken her throughout the United States and aboard. In 2018 she launched her next business Simply Tresniece, LLC. A ministry that will focus on women, inside and outside. Simply Tresniece, LLC will encourage women no matter their past, present or future to: Acknowledge Embrace and Strut Like A Queen™.

Following her passion in 2013, she started her own business Divine Faces Make-Up as Professional Make-up Artist. She has over five years' experience in the field of makeup. Her experience has afforded her the opportunity to be the MUA (Makeup Artist) for weddings, photoshoots, commercials and print work and many other special occasions. Ms. Perry has experience with various types of skin and ethnicities. Due to her expertise she has traveled to do makeup in other states and most recently traveled internationally for makeup artistry.

Rev. Tresniece is a faithful member of the Cornerstone Peaceful Bible Baptist Church, where she has been a member since the tender age of 10. At the age of 12, Rev. Tresniece accepted the Lord as her Lord and Savior and was filled with Holy Spirit. She would be 16 when she received her public call to ministry, but it would not be until the age of 24 when she would accept the call.

After completing her ministerial training under the leadership of Pastor Daniel Mangrum she was licensed to minister the Gospel in October 2007. In January 2014, she was ordained as an Associate Pastor. Rev. Tresniece feels that she has been placed in this world "for such a time as this" (Esther 4:14) to tell women, teens, and all that would listen that they matter, and that God loves them. She desires above all else that God's people know their true worth and position in God's kingdom.

Currently, Rev. Tresniece is an Associate Pastor at Cornerstone Peaceful Bible Church under the pastoral ship of Pastors Daniel and Sabrina Mangrum. The once rebellious teenager has now become an active member of CPBBC youth department, W.O.R.D ministry, Outreach, serves as a Sunday School teacher for the Woman's New Life Class as well as several other ministries at CPBBC.

Rev. Tresniece life theme is LOVE because when she was at her lowest God showed her the GREATEST amount of love. One of her favorite scriptures in the bible is Jeremiah 29:11 "for I know the plans I have for your, declares the Lord plans to prosper you and not to harm you, plans to give you a hope and future". Her response to God and HIS will for her life is simple: YES, GOD to whatever you what to me to do, wherever you want me to go, and yes to whatever you want me to say. God my heart answer is YES!

She has presented at various Women's conferences and has conducted workshops and seminars covering of topics such as emotional wellness for woman, makeup application, and spiritual healing and growth. Tresniece has provided mentoring to many young women on their journey. She currently is a Sunday School teacher for the Woman of Purpose Sunday School Class.

About the Publisher
Vision to Fruition Publishing

At Vision to Fruition, we are dedicated to helping others bring their personal, business, ministry & nonprofit visions to fruition.

Whether it's as grand as a book you want to write, a business you want to start, a conference or event you want to host, a ministry you want to launch or an organization you want to start; or as small as needing a computer repair, logo design or web design; Vision to Fruition will help you walk through the process and set you up for success! At Vision to Fruition we don't have clients, we have Visionaries. We provide solutions to equip others to pursue their visions & dreams with reckless abandon.

LaKesha L. Williams is the Visionary behind Vision to Fruition's Publishing Division. LaKesha, an acclaimed author, speaker, and minister of the Gospel of Jesus Christ, was born to parents Doris & Cleo Williams in Raleigh, North Carolina in 1983. To know LaKesha is to experience a calming spirit infused with gut-wrenching laughter at unexpected times. She has a passion for giving, which is demonstrated wholeheartedly through her founding of Born Overcomers Inc. a nonprofit organization & movement dedicated to promoting the belief that we were all Born to Overcome.

LaKesha is the Lead Visionary behind Overcomers HQ, which is dedicated to helping others overcome, thrive & bring their visions to fruition. OHQ is comprised of Born Overcomers Inc., LaKesha L. Williams Ministries, Team Overcomers & Overcomers Bling.

She has authored seven books; including two bestsellers; and is also a featured co-author in Open Your G.I.F.T.S. presented by actress & comedian Kim Coles. Her highly anticipated ninth book, Hope for the Overcomers Soul is scheduled to be released in late October of 2018.

In 2015, LaKesha received the Sista's Inspiring Sista's Phenomenal Woman Award. Since then, she has gone on to become the 2016 Indie Author Legacy Award Recipient in the Author on the Rise category, a 2016 Metro Phenomenal Woman Honoree, a 2017 TDK Publishing Author of the Year nominee & the 2018 iShine Awards winner for Author of the Year.

LaKesha, as a virgin herself, is also an advocate of abstinence, purity & virginity until marriage. Currently, LaKesha resides in Southern Maryland & enjoys serving in the community, fellowshipping with her church family at The Remnant of Hope International Church in Prince Frederick Maryland under the leadership of Pastor Margo Gross and spending time with her family & friends watching movies, sharing stories & creating new memories.

In 2018 we have published seven authors, two of which were Amazon Bestsellers. We would love for you to join our family of Visionaries as well!!!

Learn more here www.vision-fruition.com